WORKING WITH THE GEOBOARD

ACTIVITIES WITH AREA – POLYGON PROPERTIES – THE COORDINATE SYSTEM – FORMULAS

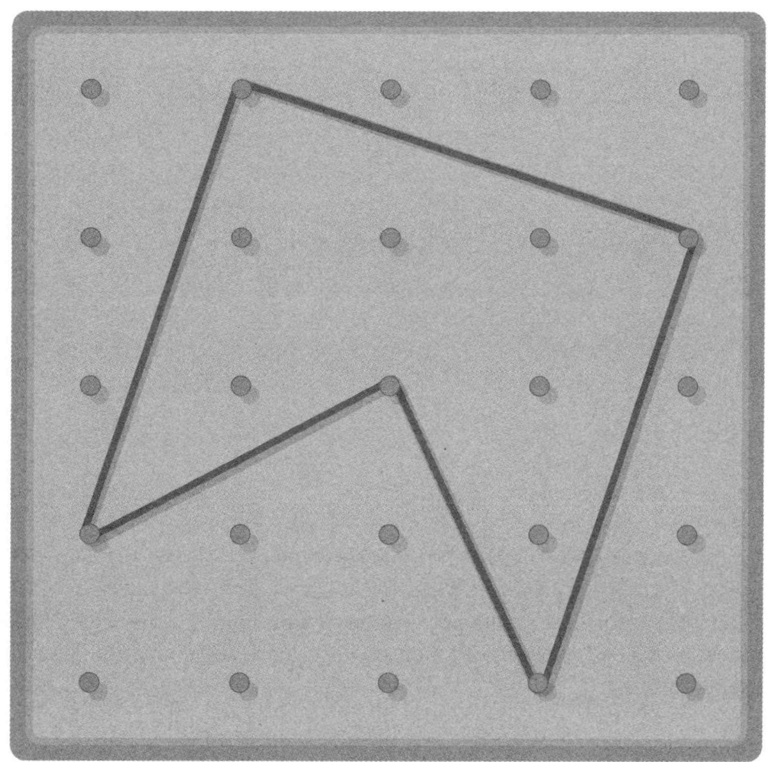

Printed in the United States of America.

Order Number 211335
ISBN 978-1-58324-350-3

A B C D E 16 15 14 13 12

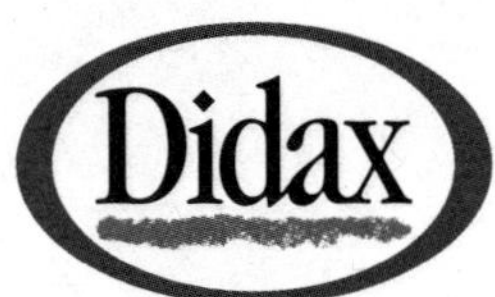

395 Main Street
Rowley, MA 01969
www.didax.com

Table of Contents

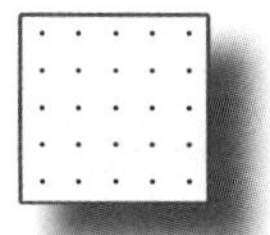

Dedication

This book is dedicated to:

My wife, Charlotte, for her encouragement and her assistance with the technology,

My dear friend Maggie Holler, who did the initial editorial work and offered encouragement and valuable ideas and suggestions,

To Cindy O'Neill for her patience, effort, and suggestions in editing the final draft of this book,

and to

The hundreds of mathematics teachers who attended my workshops and offered their valuable ideas and suggestions.

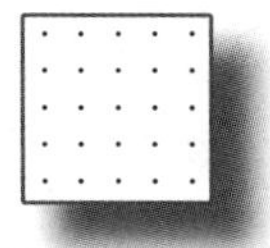

Introduction

The geoboard is a very clever educational tool, created decades ago to help teachers make geometric ideas more visual and hands-on. The geoboard comes in several different forms and compositions ranging from wood to plastic, rectangular to circular, for overhead projectors, and some with 25-pin and others with 121-pin arrays. The geoboard has a wide range of uses, from constructing very simple shapes to making many advanced algebraic and geometric concepts easier to understand, and has proven to be a useful tool for students from kindergarten through secondary school.

This book is written for the middle school level. Its purpose is to tackle many of the topics generally taught at this level in ways that help teachers become better at teaching those ideas and consequently help students better understand them. However, the ultimate goal is for students to *enjoy* learning geometry. It is hoped that by becoming more proficient in mathematics, problem solving, and deductive reasoning through the approaches presented in this book, they will do just that.

The main materials necessary to use with this book are a 25-pin geoboard, several rubber bands of different sizes and colors, a protractor, and a centimeter ruler. Since this book is intended to supplement the basal text, the lessons assume that the definitions of many geometric terms are already known.

The Structure of This Book

There are four basic parts to the lessons in this book:

1. Introduction of topics, ideas, and challenges;
2. Main Ideas: The purpose of these inserts is to provide information for those students who may be doing the activities as independent work rather than as part of a class presentation. These "main ideas" need to be presented and assimilated for the student to completely understand the lesson. The Main Idea boxes can serve as a heads-up to teachers, who sometimes assume this information is already known by the student and therefore omit it;
3. Activities for discovery, mastery, and discussion; and
4. Examples to help students better grasp the concepts and methods being presented.

Mathematics as a Science and the Role of Discovery

Piaget once wrote, "Algorithms are generalized expressions of a rule or a systematic representation of a mathematical pattern. If students can experience the rewards and motivation of their own discoveries leading up to an algorithm, mathematics can come alive for them and they will want to further study mathematics. If not, mathematics can become a laborious task of memorizing a set of meaningless rules."

This author agrees one hundred percent with Piaget's position and, therefore, this book will emphasize the discovery approach. Furthermore, a good definition of mathematics is that MATHEMATICS IS THE SCIENCE OF PATTERN AND RELATIONSHIPS. As a science, mathematics should involve four phases:

1. Experimentation, explorations, investigations (all basically the same)
2. Observations
3. Drawing conclusions
4. Verification (proofs)

This book incorporates these four phases into the lessons as much as possible.

—Dr. Carl Seltzer

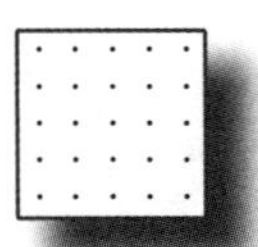

Link to the Common Core State Standards

To view a correlation of the activities in this book to the Common Core State Standards for Mathematics, please visit:

www.didax.com/211335

Chapter 1:
Finding Area on the Geoboard

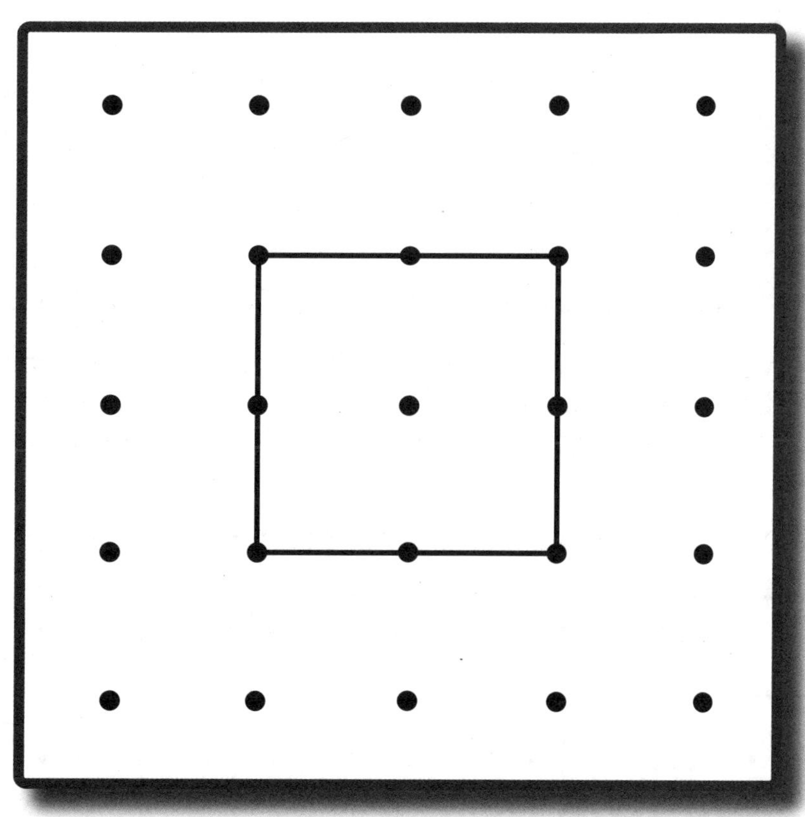

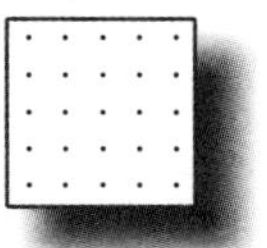

1.1 The "Rectangle Method"

Main Idea

Area is the number of square units in a shape.

It is very easy to find the area of a rectangle or square on the geoboard. One can simply count the number of square units inside the figure.

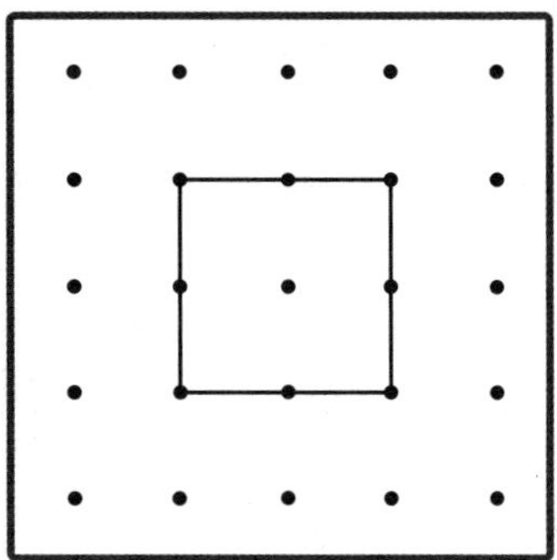

Area: 4 square units

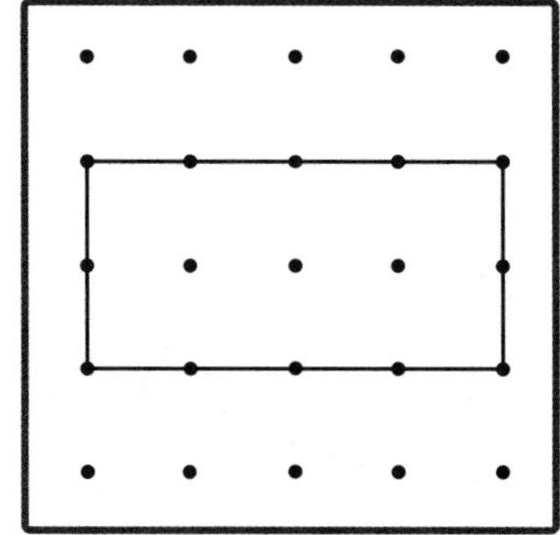

Area: 8 square units

Other polygons provide more of a challenge, but one fact of geometry can help solve that problem: A diagonal is a line that connects *nonadjacent* (not next to each other) vertices of a shape. As shown below, the diagonal of any parallelogram divides it into two equal parts, or two equal areas.

In the figures *ABCD*, *AC* is one diagonal. *DB* would be the other diagonal.

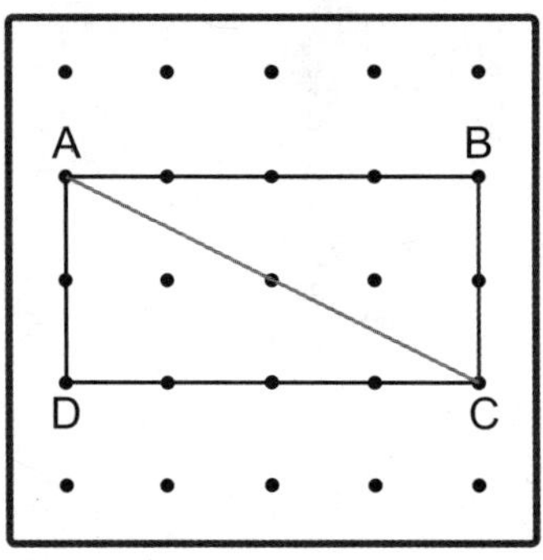

Area ABC = Area ADC

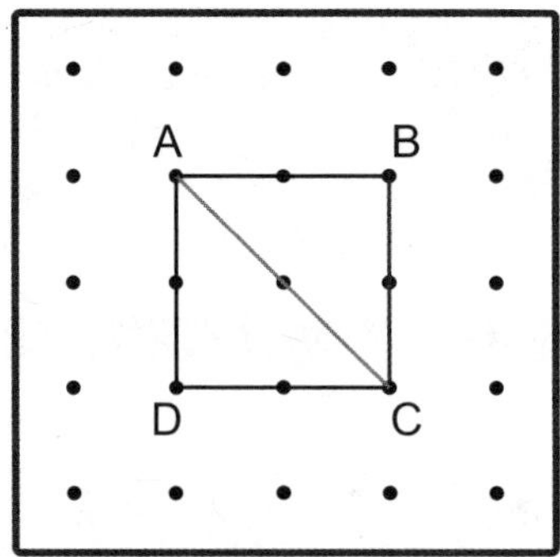

Area *ABC* = Area *ADC*

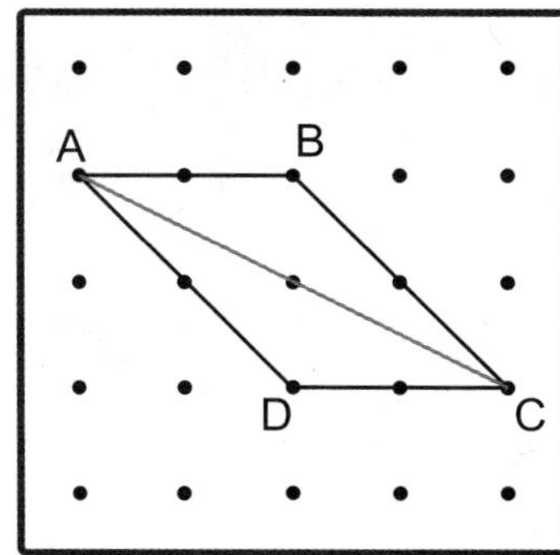

Area *ABC* = Area *ADC*

As can be seen from the third figure above, sometimes it isn't possible to simply count the number of square units to find the area. In such cases, the area can be found by constructing rectangles that include the shape for which we want to find the area.

Look at the following:

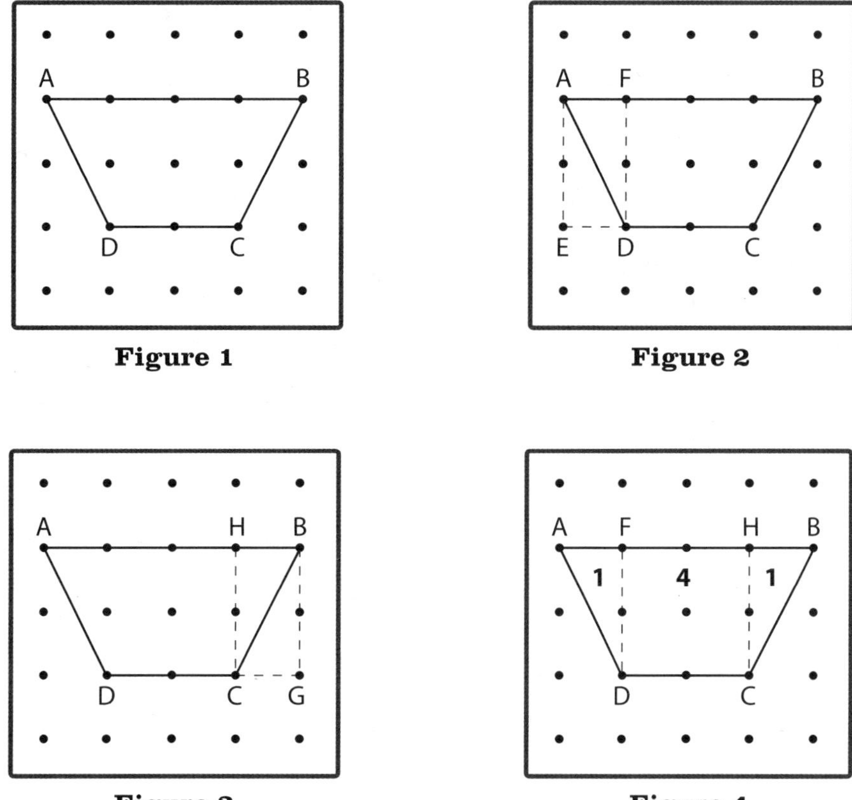

Figure 1

Figure 2

Figure 3

Figure 4

Say we want to find the area of *ABCD*, a trapezoid (Figure 1). Let's use the "rectangle method."

We can build a rectangle, *AFDE*, on one end of the trapezoid (Figure 2). Note that *AFDE* is a rectangle with an area of 2 square units.

The diagonal *AD* divides the rectangle *AFDE* into two equal parts. So the area of *ADF* = $\frac{1}{2}$ the area of *AFDE,* or 1 square unit.

Figure 3 shows the same procedure, so the area of *HBC* = 1 square unit.

FHCD, shown in Figure 4, has an area of 4 square units. Therefore, the total area of *ABCD* is 6 square units.

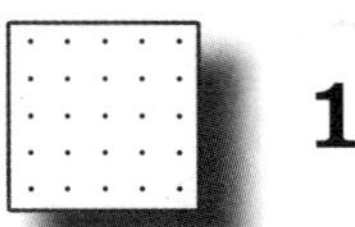

1.2 The "Chop Method"

Another method we can use to find the area of a polygon is called the "chop method." Here is an example of how the chop method works:

Take the figure *ABCD,* an irregular polygon:

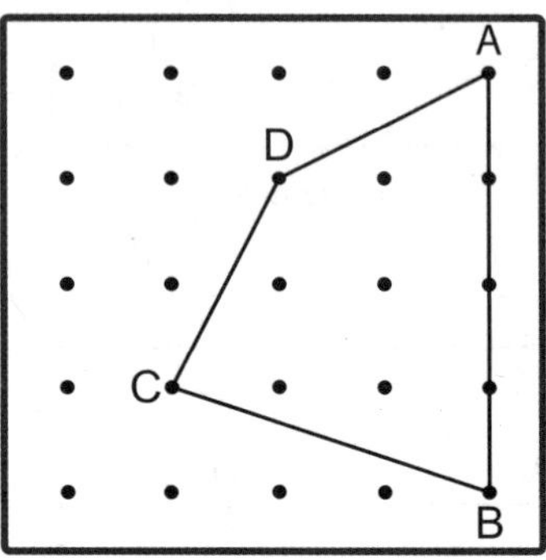

Step 1:

Build a rectangle completely around the shape. Note that the area of this rectangle, *FABE*, is 12 square units.

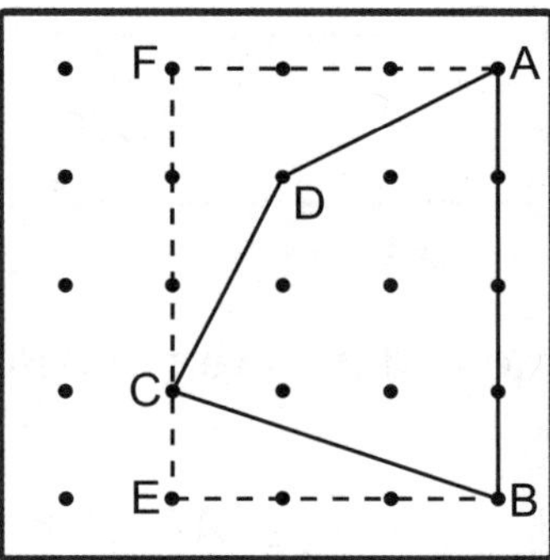

Step 2:

Begin chopping:

Area of *GAD* = $\frac{1}{2}$ area of *GAJD* = 1 square unit.

Area of *HDC* = $\frac{1}{2}$ area of *HDKC* = 1 square unit.

Area of *CBE* = $\frac{1}{2}$ area of *CLBE* = $1\frac{1}{2}$ square units.

Area of *FGDH* = 1 square unit.

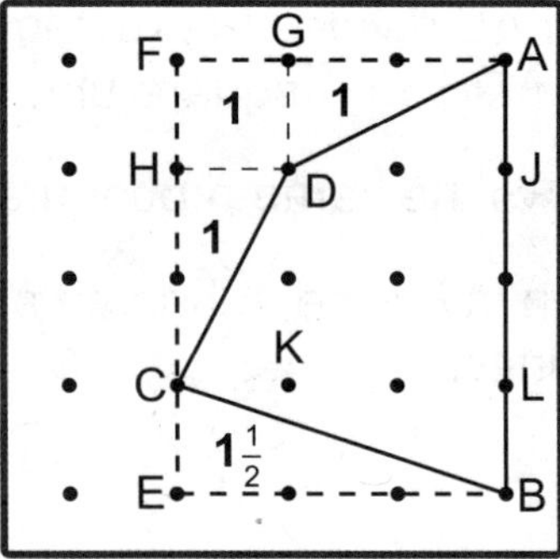

Altogether, this chops $4\frac{1}{2}$ square units off the 12-square-unit rectangle *FABE*.

This means the area of the original polygon *ABCD* is $7\frac{1}{2}$ square units.

PRACTICE

Name: ______________________ Date: ______________________

Find the Area Using the "Rectangle Method"

Make these shapes on your geoboard and find their areas.

1.

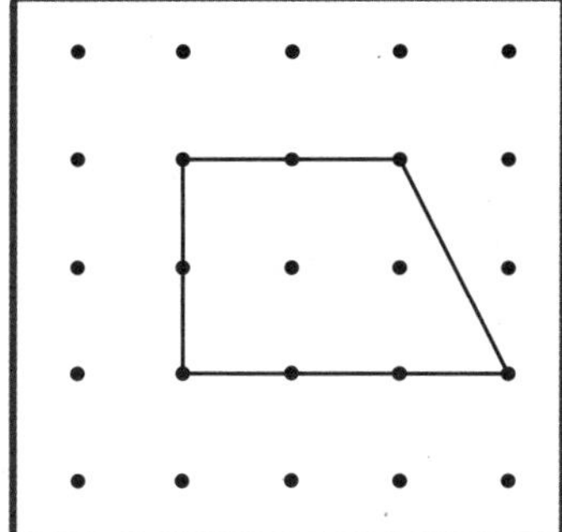

Area = ________ sq. units

2.

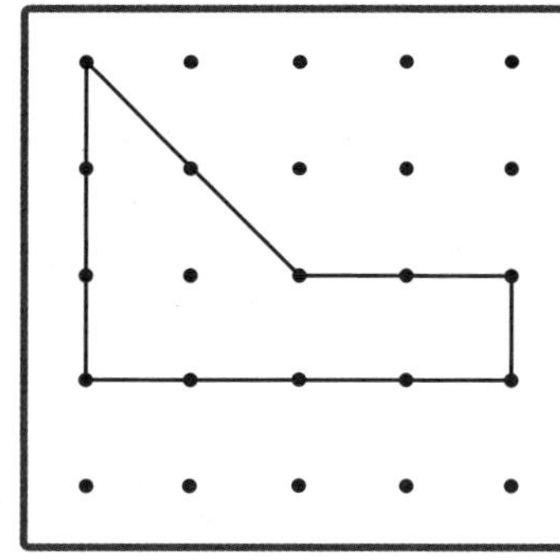

Area = ________ sq. units

3.

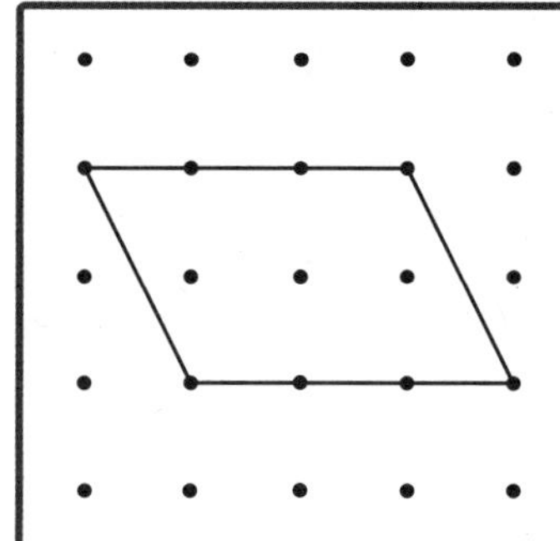

Area = ________ sq. units

4.

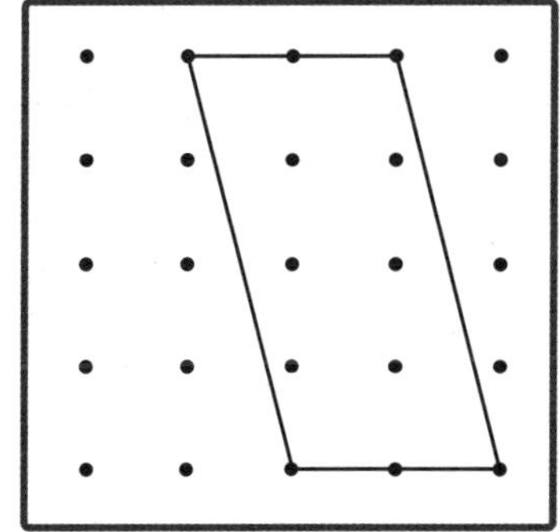

Area = ________ sq. units

5.

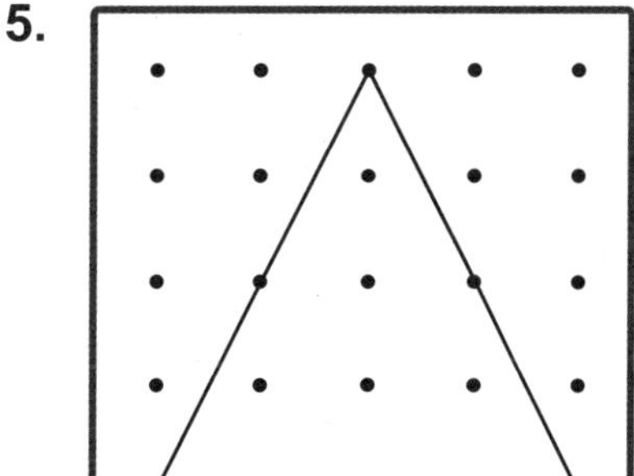

Area = ________ sq. units

6.

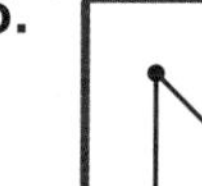

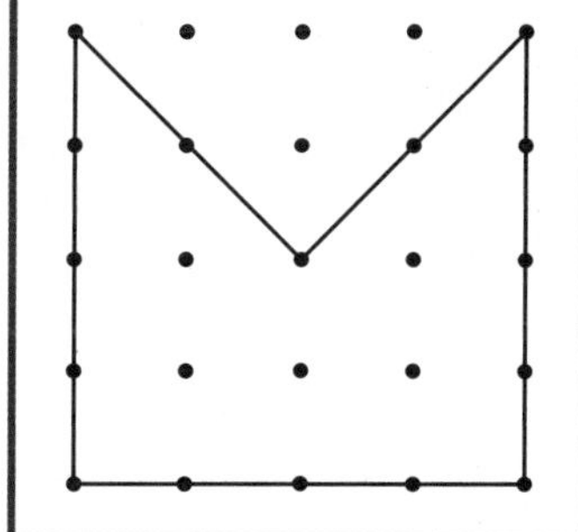

Area = ________ sq. units

7.

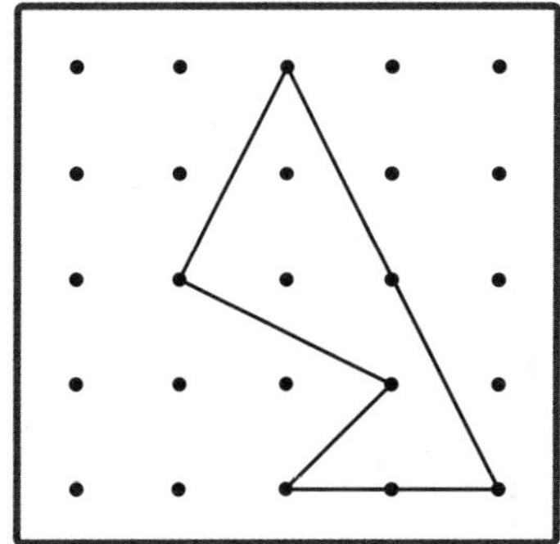

Area = ________ sq. units

8.

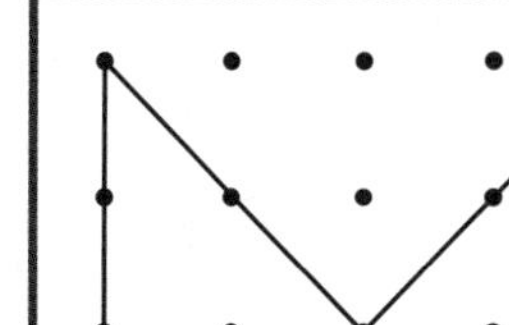

Area = ________ sq. units

9.

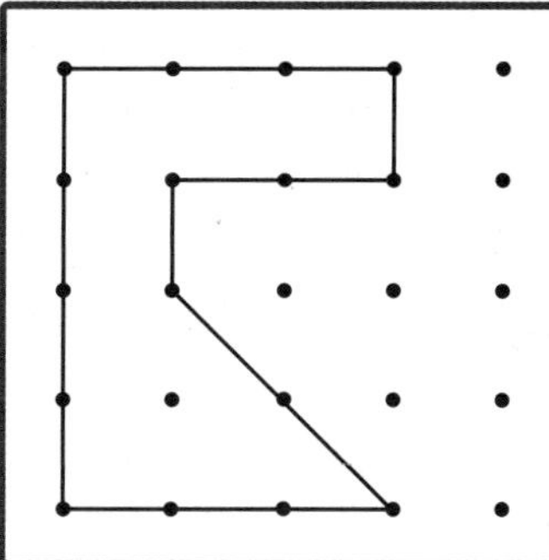

Area = ________ sq. units

Name: ______________________ Date: ______________________

Find the Area Using the "Chop Method"

Make these shapes on your geoboard and find their areas.

Example:

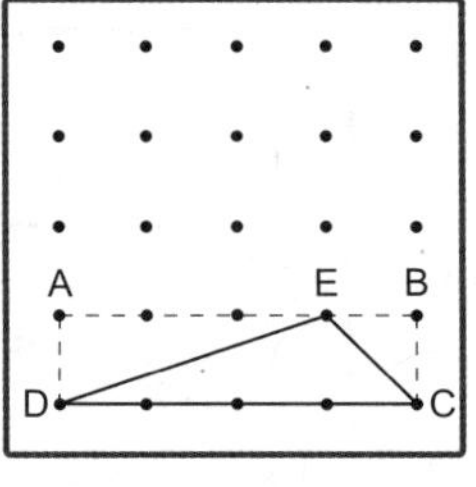

Area of *ABCD* = 4

– Area of *AED* = $1\frac{1}{2}$

– Area of *EBC* = $\frac{1}{2}$

Area of *DEC* = 2

1.

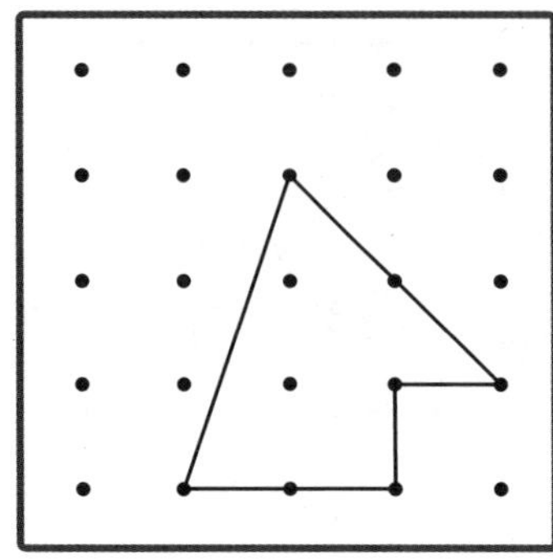

Area = __________ sq. units

2.

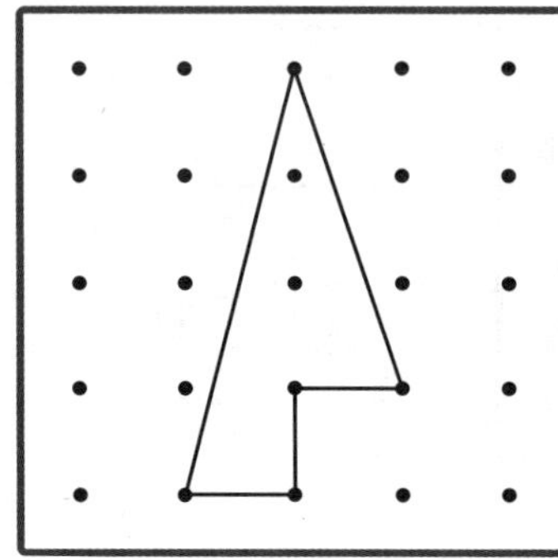

Area = __________ sq. units

3.

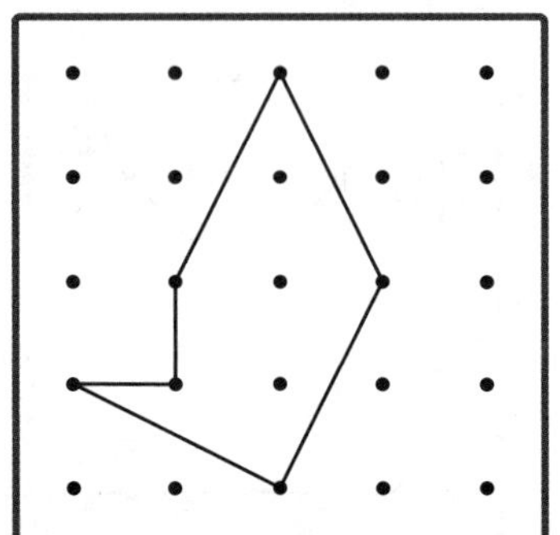

Area = __________ sq. units

4.

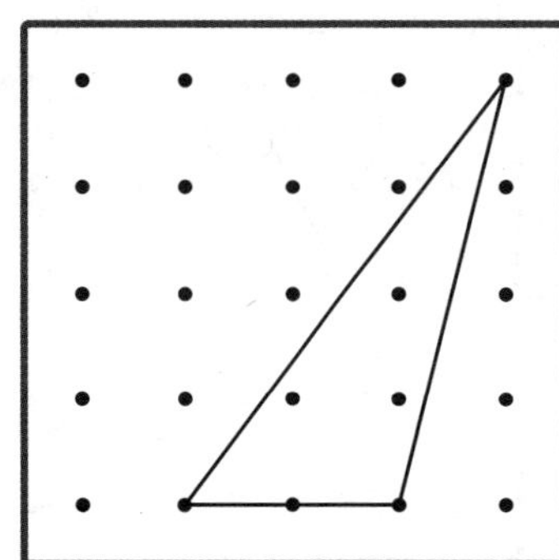

Area = __________ sq. units

5.

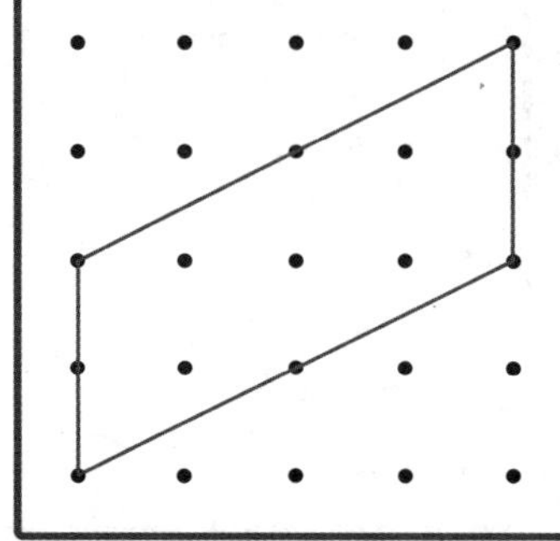

Area = __________ sq. units

6.

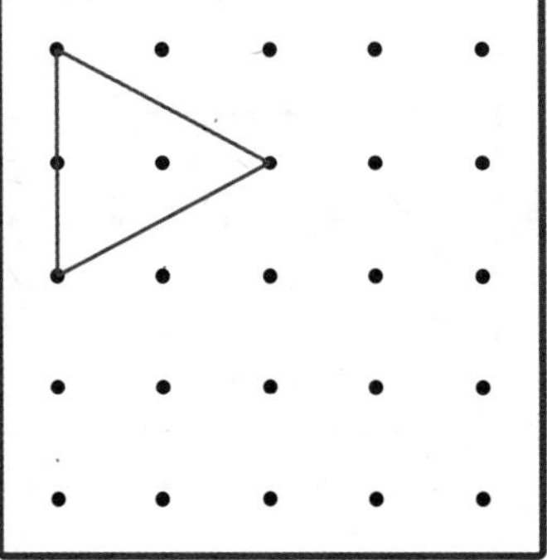

Area = __________ sq. units

7.

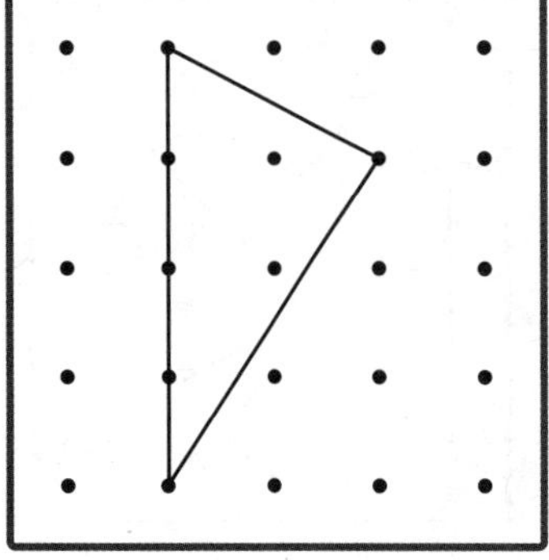

Area = __________ sq. units

8.

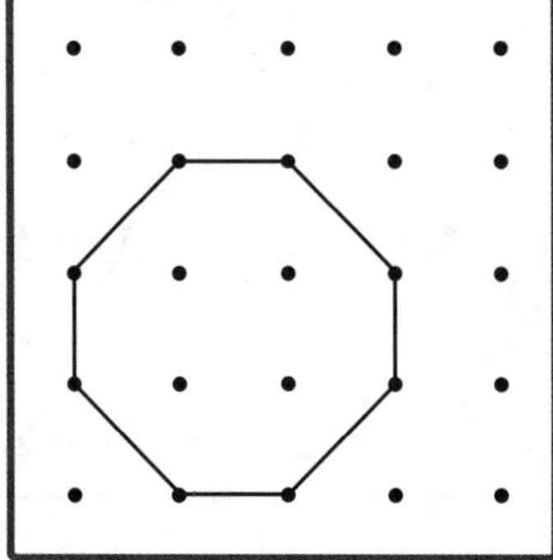

Area = __________ sq. units

Name: ____________________ Date: ____________________

Find the Area

Make these shapes on your geoboard and find their areas using either the rectangle method or the chop method.

1.

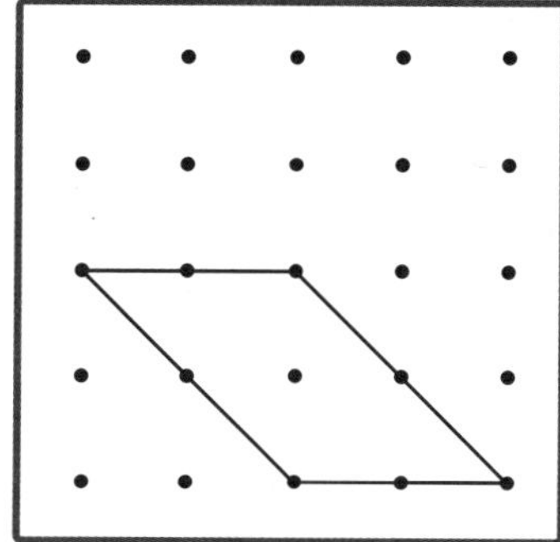

Area = ________ sq. units

2.

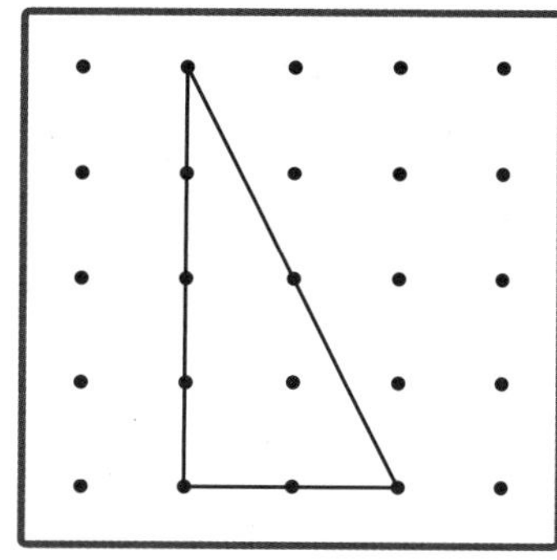

Area = ________ sq. units

3.

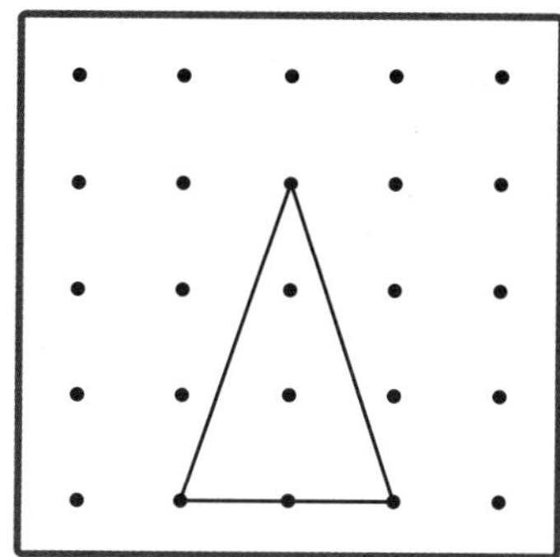

Area = ________ sq. units

4.

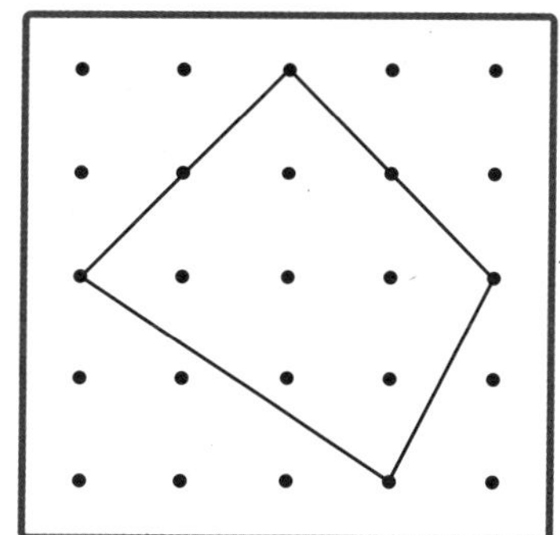

Area = ________ sq. units

5.

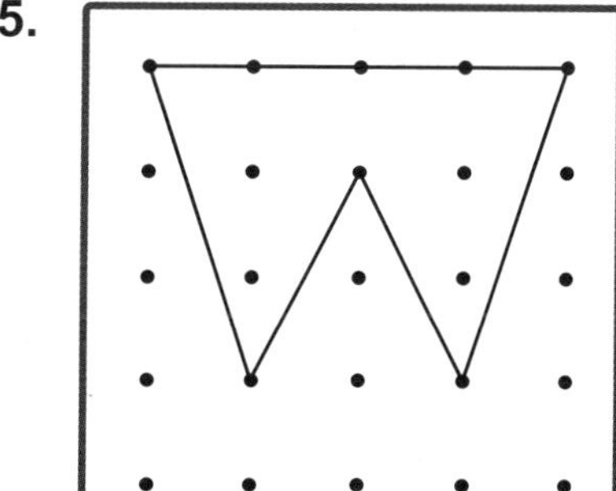

Area = ________ sq. units

6.

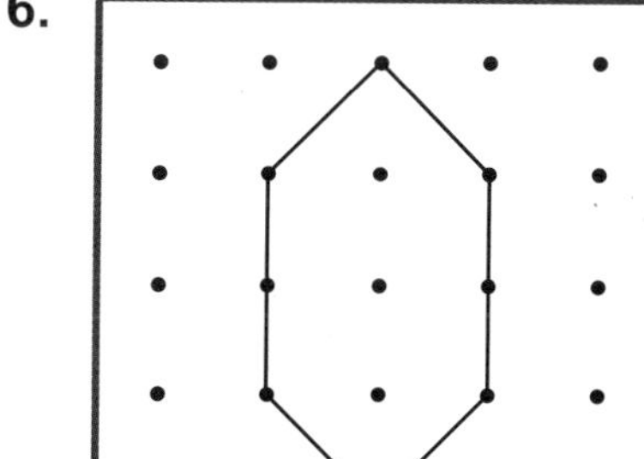

Area = ________ sq. units

7.

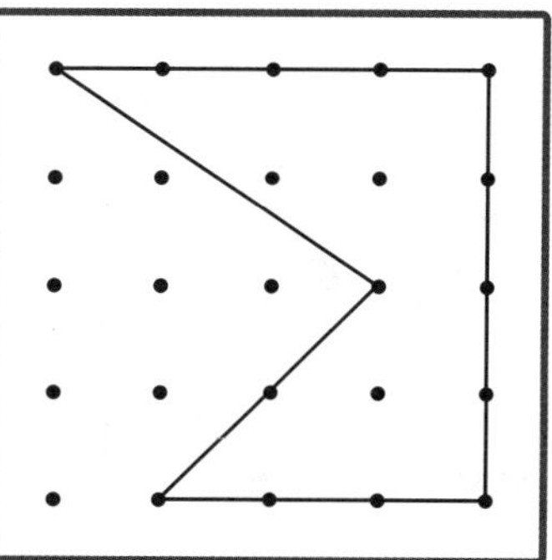

Area = ________ sq. units

8.

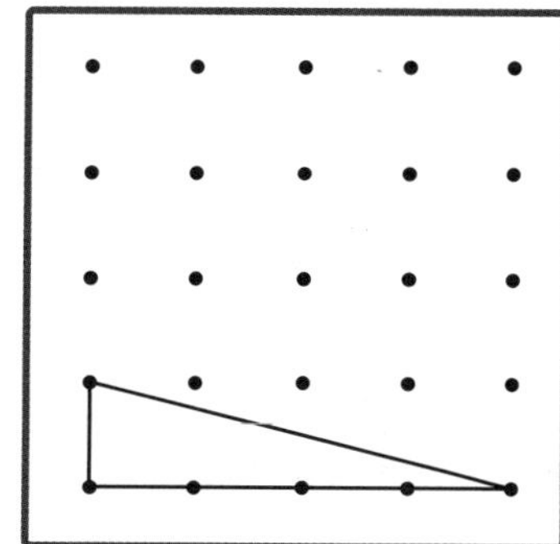

Area = ________ sq. units

9.

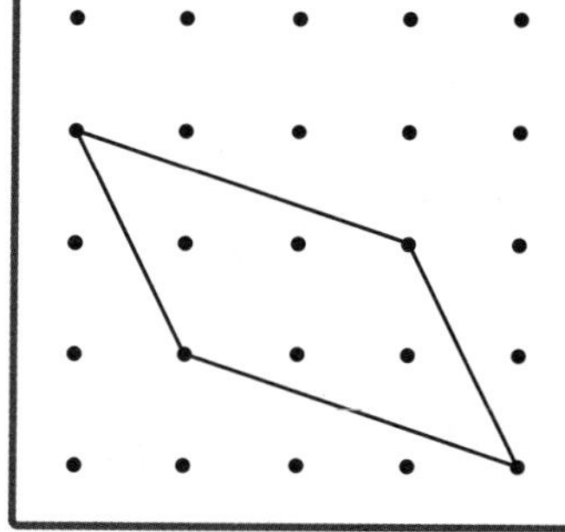

Area = ________ sq. units

Name: ______________________ Date: ______________________

What's the Area?

Make a shape on your geoboard—any shape you want. Find the area of the shape you made. Sketch your shape on the blank geoboard below if it will help.

Ask a classmate to find the area of your shape. If you disagree on what the area is, look at your solutions together to determine the correct answer.

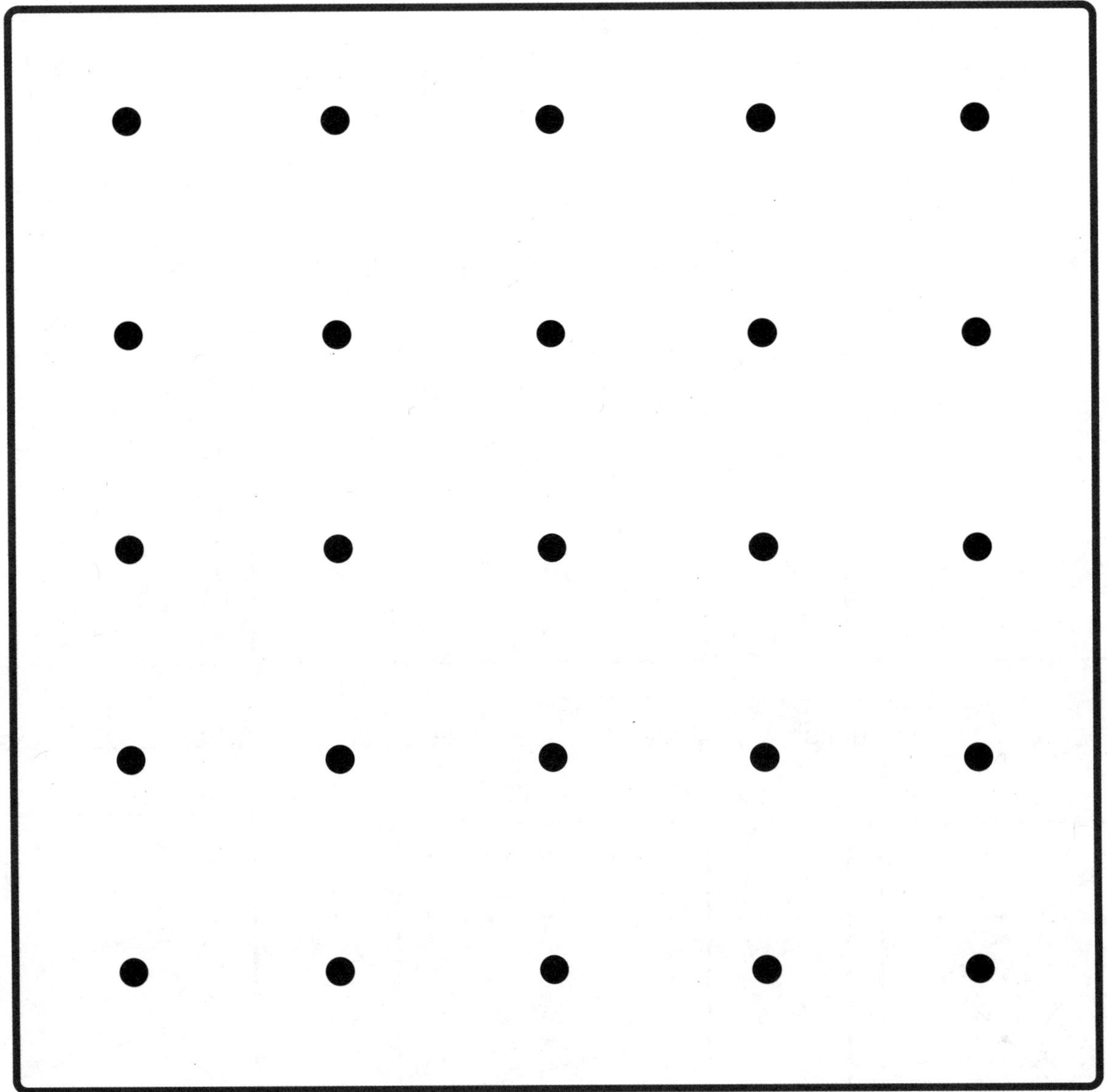

Chapter 2:
Exploring Shapes with the Geoboard

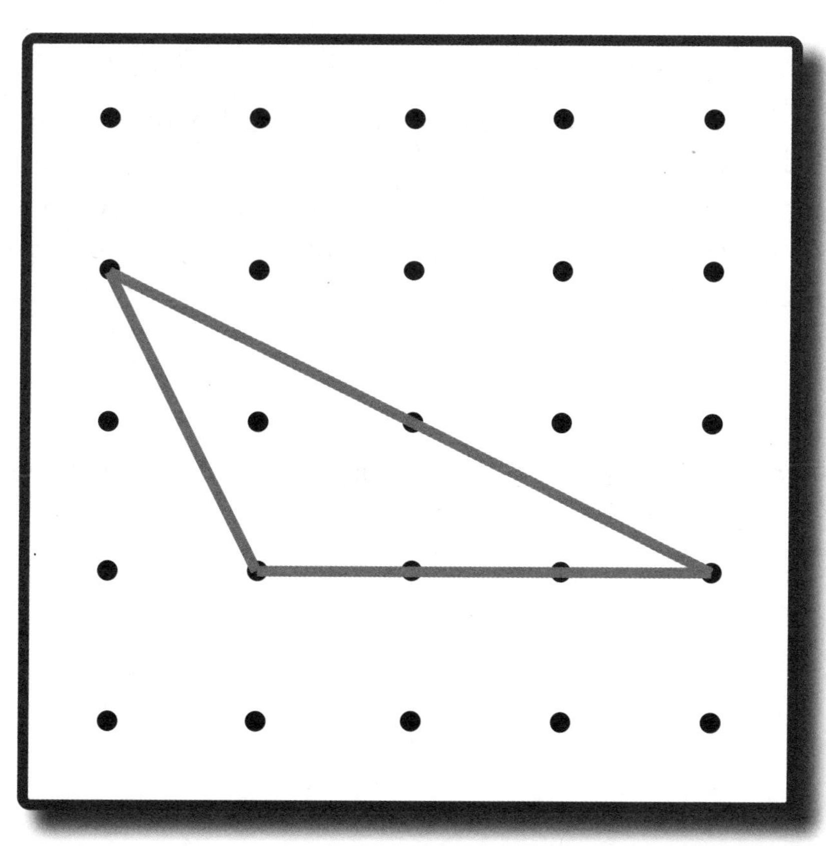

2.1 Properties of Triangles

Main Ideas

A *triangle* is a polygon with three sides and is classified by the measures of its angles or the lengths of its sides. If classified by the lengths of its sides, a triangle is called *scalene, isosceles,* or *equilateral:*

Scalene – No two sides are equal in length.

Isosceles – At least two sides are equal in length.

Equilateral – All three sides are equal in length.

If classified by the measures of its angles, a triangle is called *acute, obtuse,* or *right*:

Acute – An acute triangle has three acute angles. *Acute* means less than 90 degrees, or less than a right angle.

Obtuse – An obtuse triangle has one obtuse angle. *Obtuse* means greater than 90 degrees. *Obtuse* means greater than 90 degrees but less than 180 degrees.

Right – A right triangle has one right angle—that is, an angle of 90 degrees.

Equiangular – All angles are equal in measure.

Have students use their geoboards to explore the properties of triangles in the activities that follow.

Name: ____________________ Date: ____________________

Scalene, Isosceles, and Equilateral Triangles

Use your geoboard to make the triangles on this page, and complete the table on the next page. (Hint: Fill in the corresponding row of the table as you make each triangle.)

A

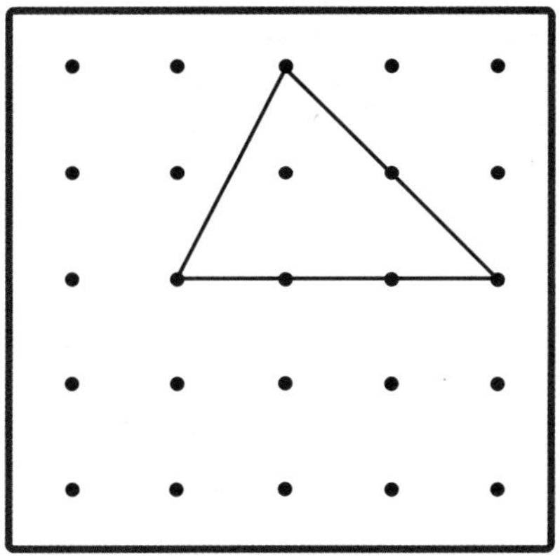

B

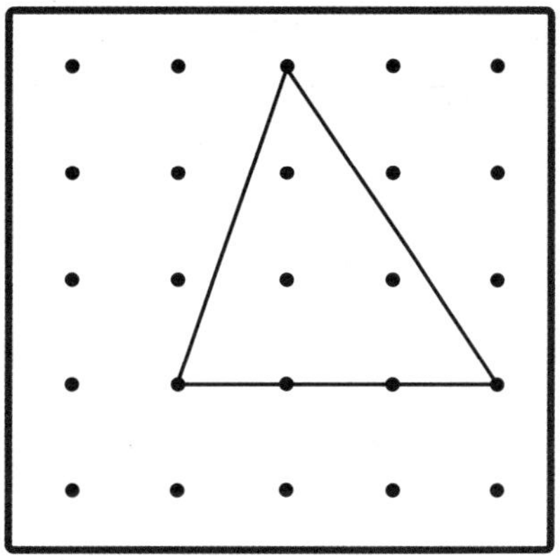

C

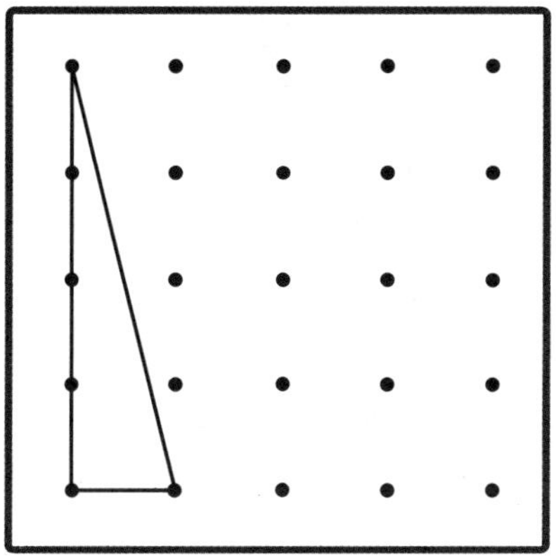

D

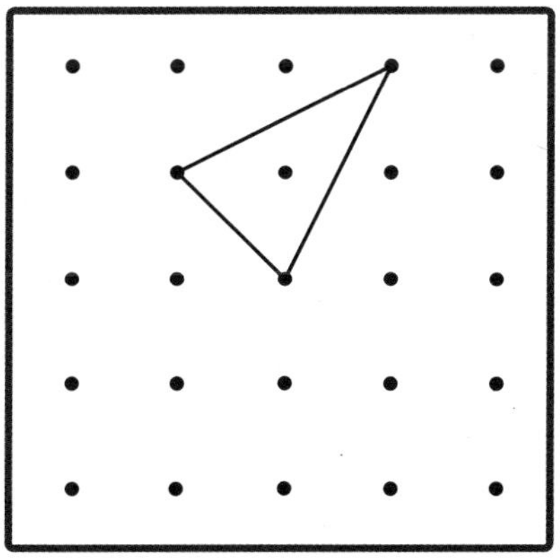

E

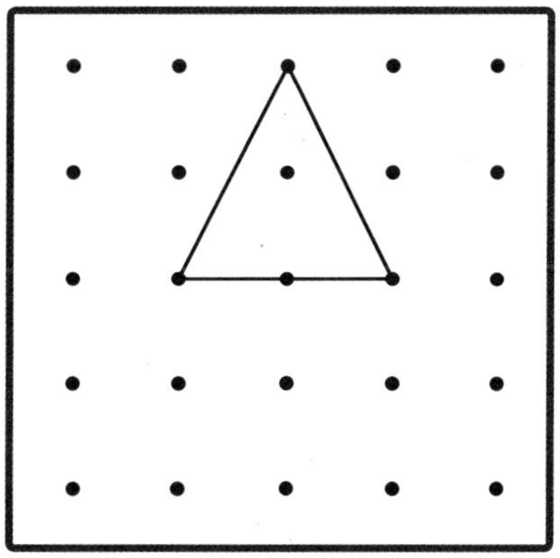

F

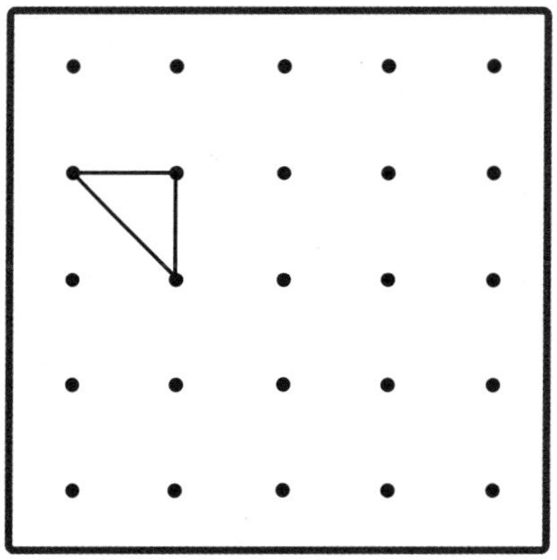

G

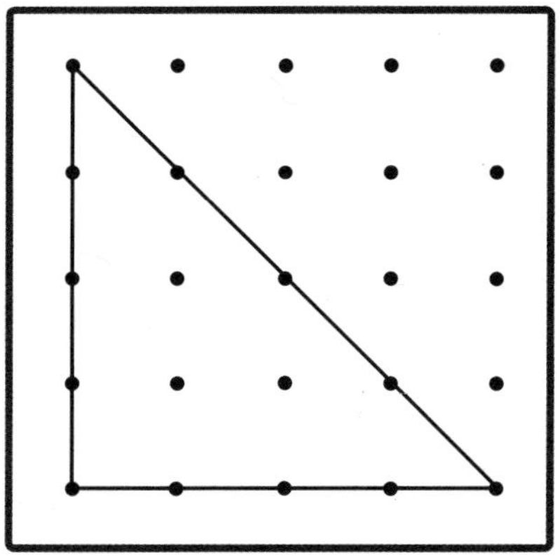

H

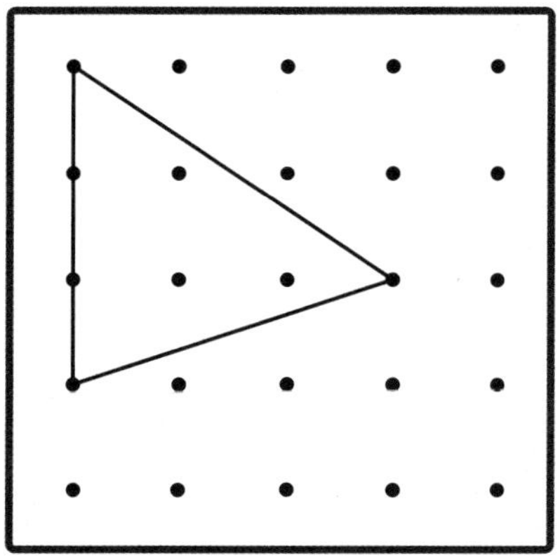

I

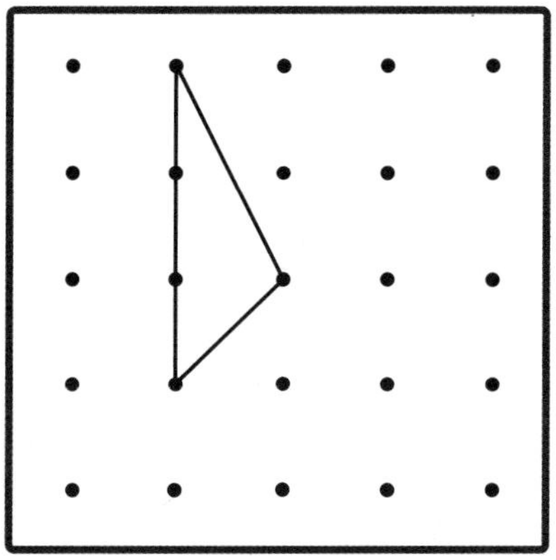

Name: ______________________________ Date: ______________________

Scalene, Isosceles, and Equilateral Triangles (cont.)

Refer to the triangles on the previous page and complete the following table. Measure the lengths of the sides with your ruler.

Shape	# Pegs Inside	Scalene	Isosceles	Equilateral
A				
B				
C				
D				
E				
F				
G				
H				
I				

Name: ______________________ Date: ______________________

Triangles

Use your geoboard to make the triangles on this page, and complete the table on the next page. (Hint: Fill in each row of the table as you make each triangle.)

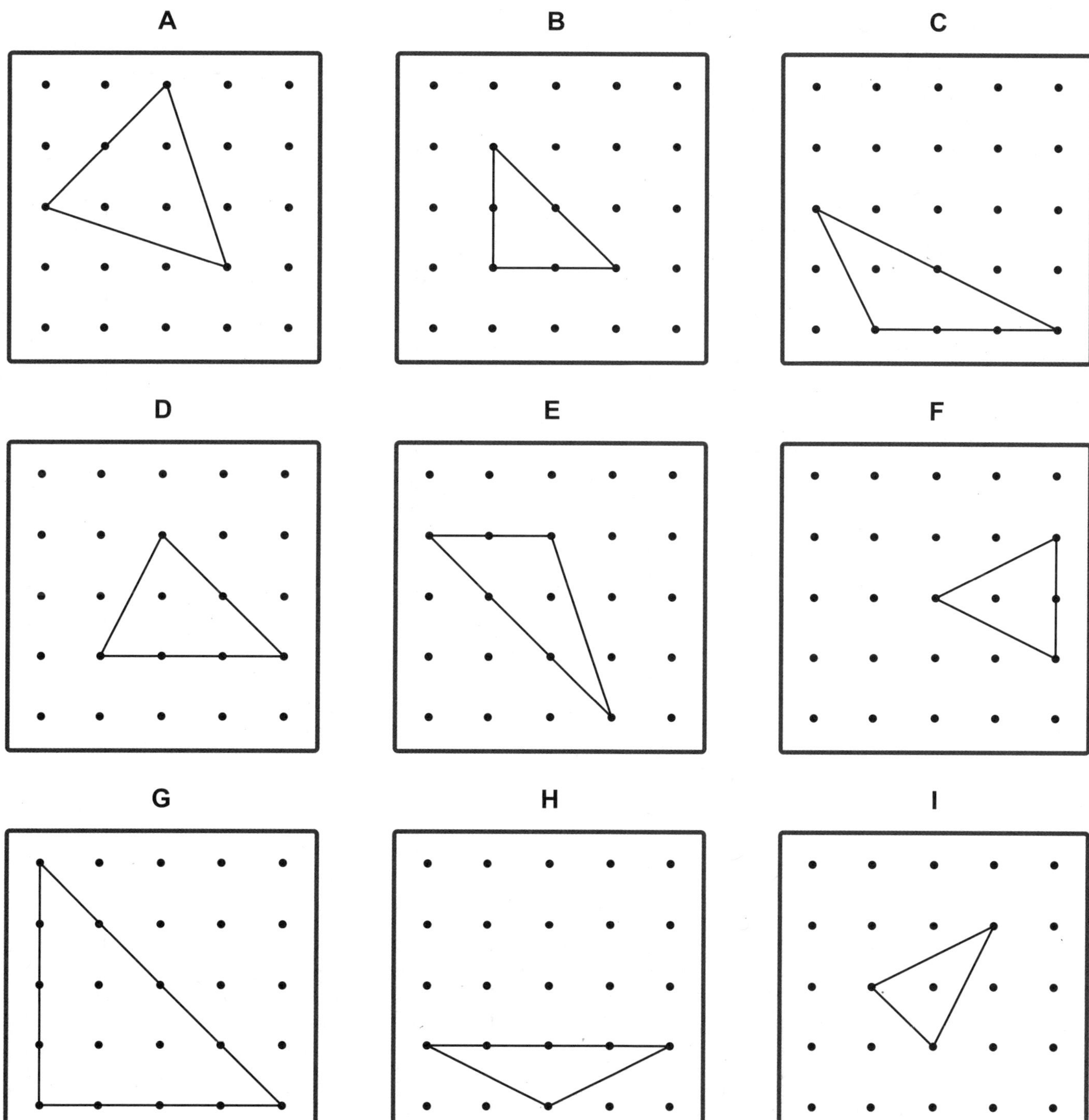

Name: ______________________ Date: ______________________

Triangles (cont.)

Refer to the triangles on the previous page and complete the this table. Classify each triangle by its angles and then by its side lengths.

Shape	# Pegs Inside	Acute	Obtuse	Right	Isosceles	Scalene	Equilateral
A							
B							
C							
D							
E							
F							
G							
H							
I							

Name: ______________________________ Date: ______________________

Triangles

Look back at the tables on pages 12 and 14 and answer the following questions. Circle the correct answer. (You may need to make the triangles on your geoboard again to solve these problems.)

1. Are all isosceles triangles acute triangles? **Yes** **No**

2. Are all scalene triangles acute triangles? **Yes** **No**

3. Can you make a right triangle that is isosceles on your geoboard? **Yes** **No**

4. Can you make a right triangle that is obtuse? **Yes** **No**

5. Can you make a right acute triangle? **Yes** **No**

6. Are all right triangles acute? **Yes** **No**

7. Is it possible to make an equilateral triangle on your 25-pin geoboard? **Yes** **No**

8. Triangles with pegs inside are always larger in area than triangles without pegs inside. **True** **False**

9. Right triangles cannot have pegs inside. **True** **False**

10. Acute triangles are always smaller in area than obtuse triangles. **True** **False**

2.2 Properties of Quadrilaterals

Main Ideas

A *quadilateral* is a four-sided closed shape. *Parallelograms*—squares, rectangles, rhombi (plural of *rhombus*), and trapezoids—are the most common types of quadrilaterals.

Parallelogram – A quadrilateral whose opposite sides are parallel

Rectangle – A parallelogram with four right angles

Rhombus – A parallelogram with four sides equal in length

Square – A rectangle with four sides equal in length

Trapezoid – A quadrilateral with exactly one pair of parallel sides

NOTE: A rectangle actually has 4 right angles, as does a square. Generally, definitions include only the bare essentials to determine the meaning. Other characteristics can be proven in the form of theorems.

In the activities that follow, students use their geoboards to explore the properties of each of these quadrilaterals.

Name: ____________________ Date: ____________________

When Is a Rhombus Not a Rhombus?

Here is a shape that looks like a rhombus. Make the shape on your geoboard, and determine whether it is really a rhombus according to the definition of a rhombus.

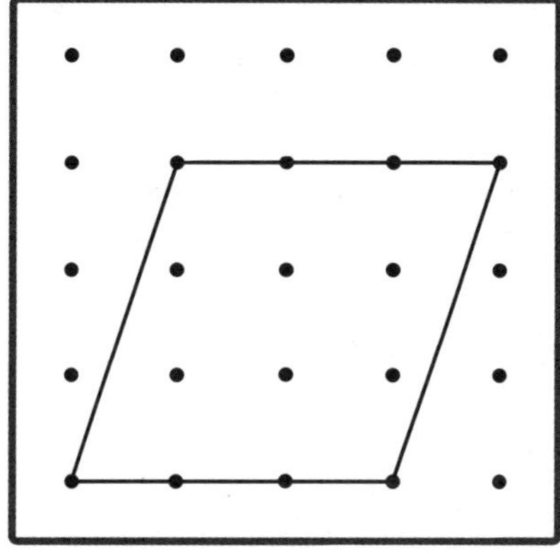

Is this shape a rhombus? __________ Why or why not? ____________________

____

____

____

Name: ______________________________ Date: ______________________

Quadrilaterals

Use your geoboard to answer the following questions.

1. Name three characteristics of a square.

A. ____

B. ____

C. ____

2. Name three characteristics of a rectangle.

A. ____

B. ____

C. ____

3. Name three characteristics of a trapezoid.

A. ____

B. ____

C. ____

4. Name three characteristics of a rhombus.

A. ____

B. ____

C. ____

5. Is it possible to make a rhombus on your geoboard? **Yes** **No**

6. Is it possible to make a square with an area equal to the area of a rhombus?

Yes, but not on the geoboard **No**

7. Can the area of a square ever equal the area of a triangle? **Yes** **No**

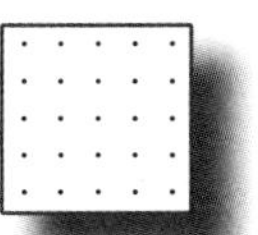

2.3 Other Polygons

Main Ideas

There are many geometric shapes other than those we have studied so far. Here are the names of some of the other shapes:

Pentagon – A polygon with 5 sides

Hexagon – A polygon with 6 sides

Heptagon – A polygon with 7 sides

Octagon – A polygon with 8 sides

Nonagon – A polygon with 9 sides

Decagon – A polygon with 10 sides

A *regular polygon* is a shape with all sides and all angles congruent. *Congruent* means that all sides are the same length and all interior angles have the same measure.

An *irregular polygon* is a polygon whose sides are not all the same length and whose interior angles do not all have the same measure. In other words, the interior angles of an irregular polygon are not congruent, nor are the sides. Irregular polygons can be classified as *convex* or *concave*.

Rather than defining the terms *convex* and *concave* for students, see whether they can discover the meanings of these terms as they work through the following activity on irregular polygons.

Name: ______________________ Date: ______________________

Concave or Convex?

Look at the four polygons shown below. Some are *concave* and some are *convex.* Then answer the questions.

A

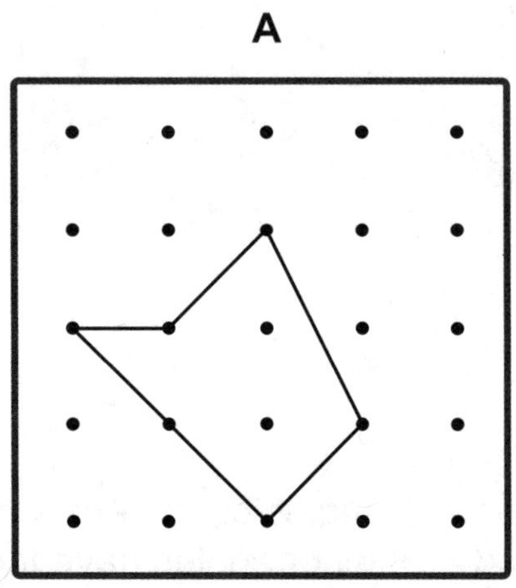

B

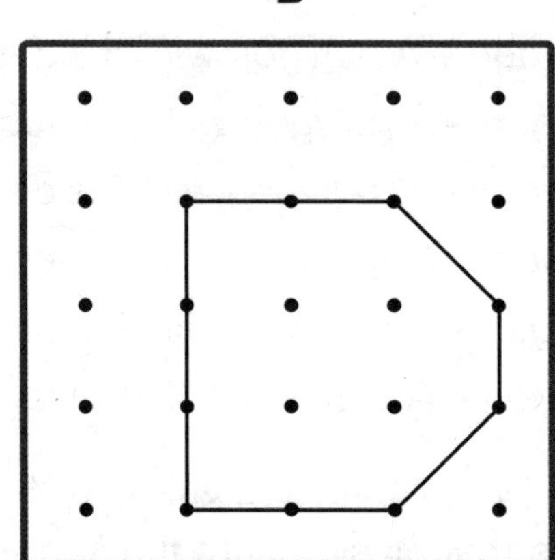

C

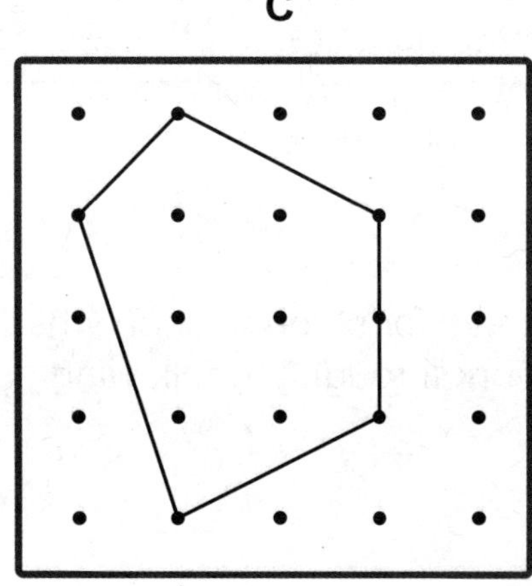

D

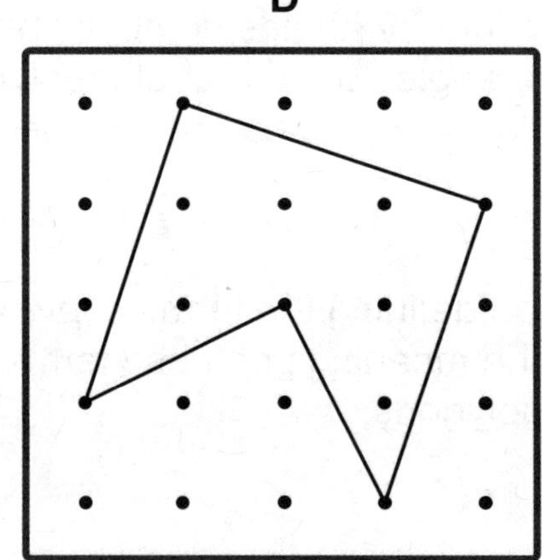

Which do you think are conCAVE? ______________________

Which do you think are convex? ______________________

CHECK YOUR UNDERSTANDING

Name: ______________________ Date: ______________________

Polygons

Circle the correct answers.

1.	All squares are rectangles.	**True**	**False**
2.	All rectangles are squares.	**True**	**False**
3.	The diagonal of *any* polygon divides it into two equal areas.	**True**	**False**
4.	All rhombi are parallelograms.	**True**	**False**
5.	All parallelograms are quadrilaterals.	**True**	**False**
6.	Trapezoids have two pairs of parallel sides.	**True**	**False**
7.	All octagons are regular shapes.	**True**	**False**
8.	A heptagon always has seven sides.	**True**	**False**
9.	All triangles are polygons.	**True**	**False**
10.	The greatest area you can make on your 25-pin geoboard is 25 square units.	**True**	**False**
11.	The smallest area you can make on your geoboard is $\frac{1}{2}$ square unit.	**True**	**False**
12.	The chop method is most useful for irregular shapes.	**True**	**False**
13.	A rhombus always has two obtuse angles.	**True**	**False**
14.	Is it possible to make a *regular* pentagon on the geoboard?	**Yes**	**No**
15.	Can a square ever have an area that is an odd number?	**Yes**	**No**

Chapter 3: Formulas and Patterns on the Geoboard

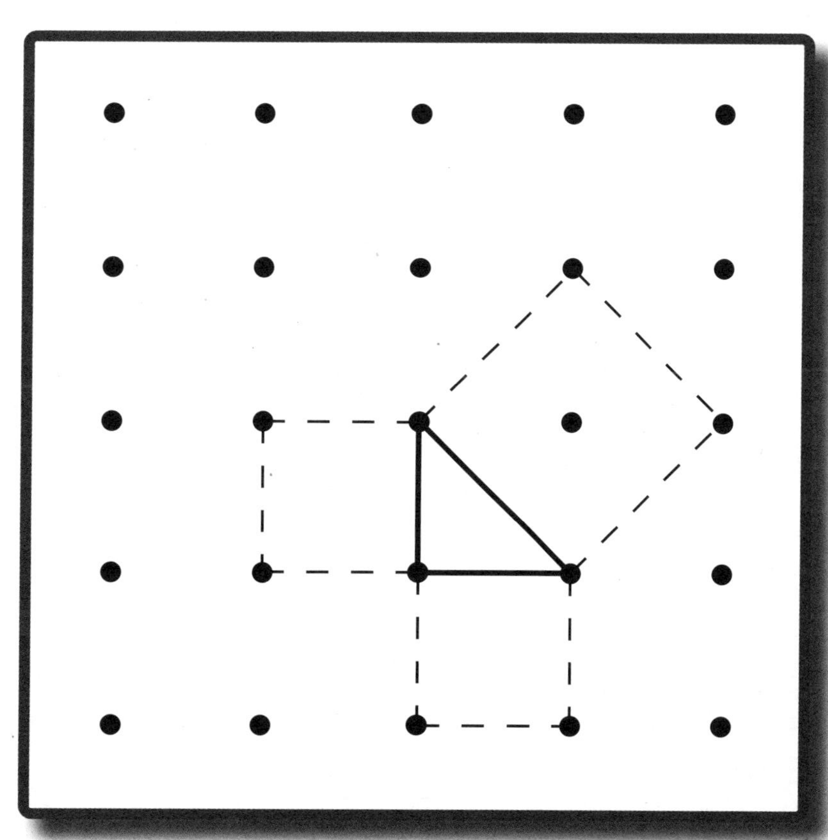

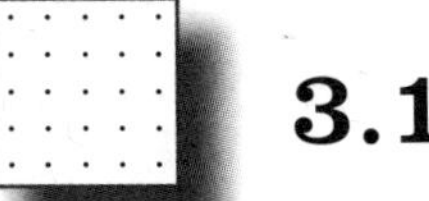

3.1 Formulas for Area

Main Idea

Formulas are discovered by looking for *patterns* and then forming *generalizations*.

In the activities that follow, students use their geoboards to discover formulas for area and perimeter for different polygons. They also take a closer look at right triangles to discover the Pythagorean Theorem for finding the length of the hypotenuse.

Name: ____________________ Date: ____________________

Area Formulas

Look at the three sets of shapes below: squares, rectangles, and triangles. Find the areas of the different shapes. Then see whether you can spot a pattern that points to the formula for area for each set of figures.

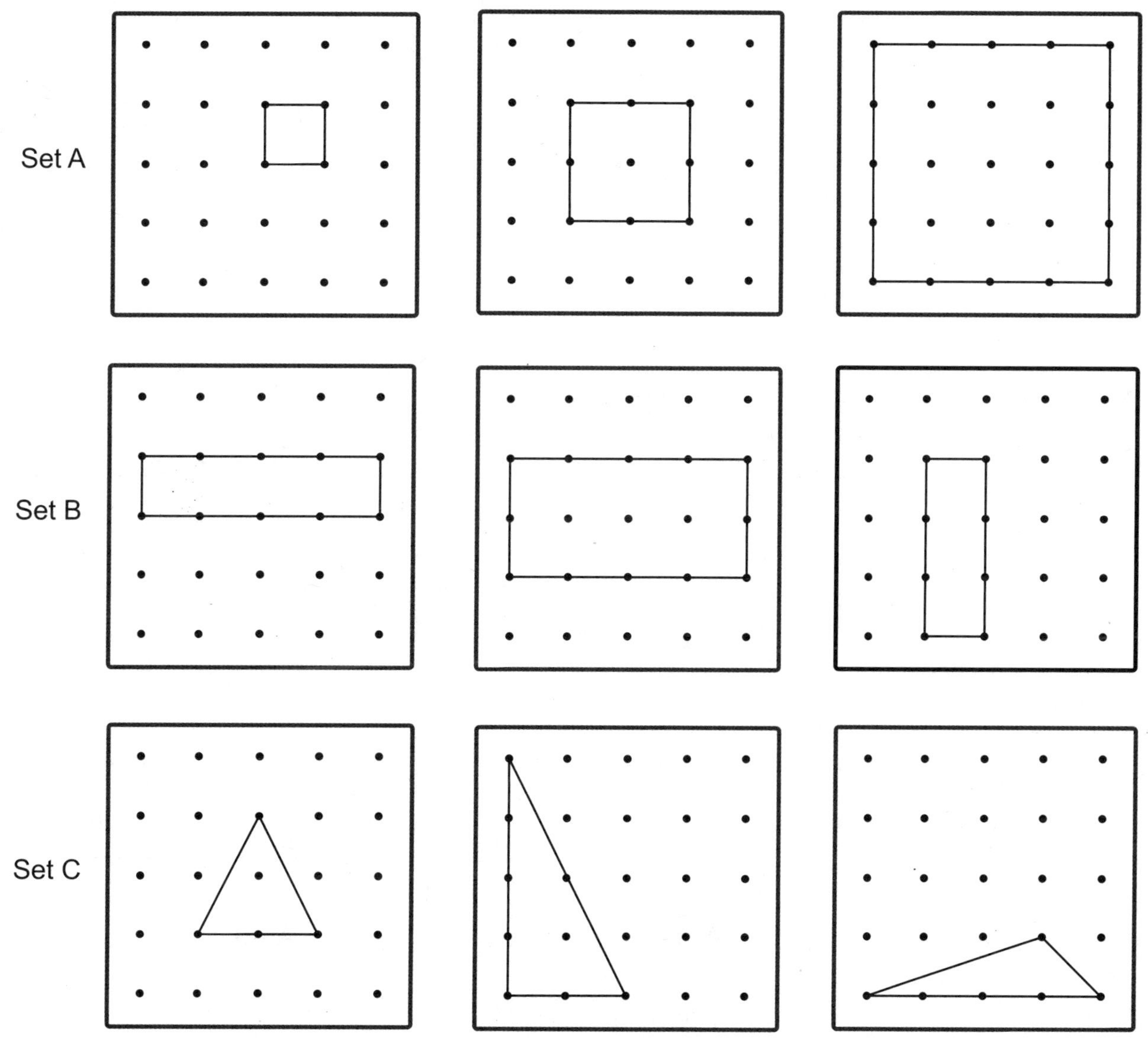

1. Set A: Area: __________ Formula: ____________________

2. Set B: Area: __________ Formula: ____________________

3. Set C: Area: __________ Formula: ____________________

Name: ______________________ Date: ______________________

More Area Formulas

Look carefully at the shapes below, looking for patterns. For each shape, find the area and then write a formula for finding the area, if you can.

1.

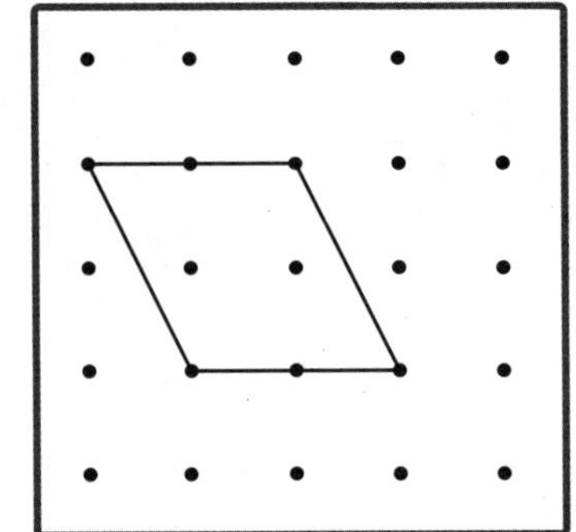

Area: ______________

Formula: ______________

2.

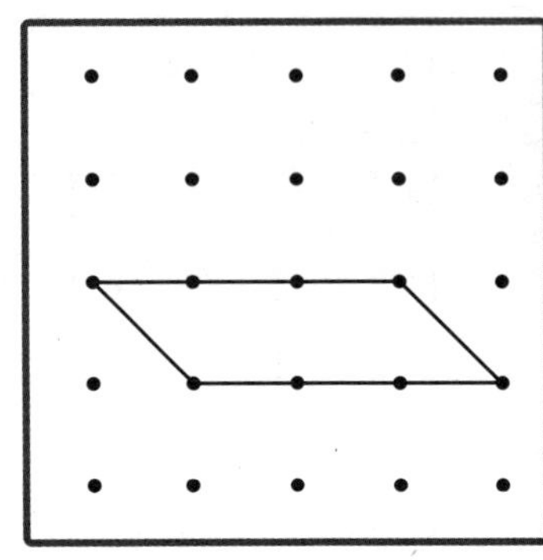

Area: ______________

Formula: ______________

3.

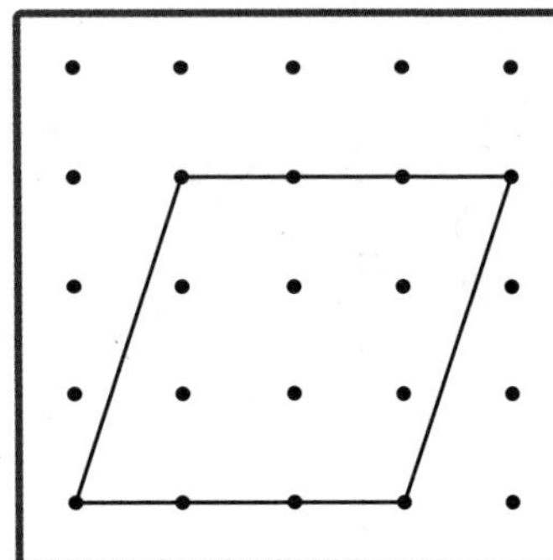

Area: ______________

Formula: ______________

4.

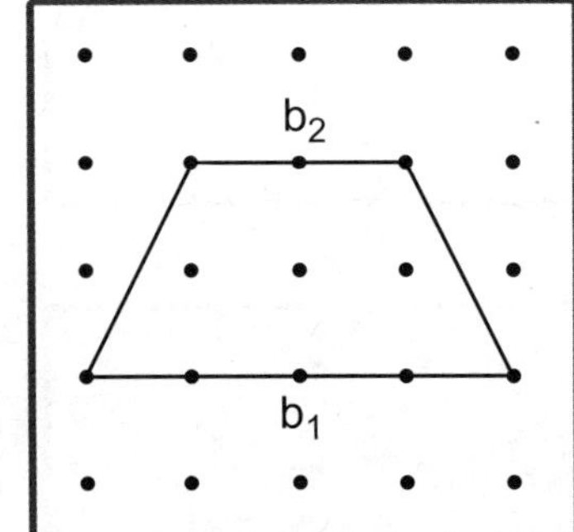

Area: ______________

Formula: ______________

5.

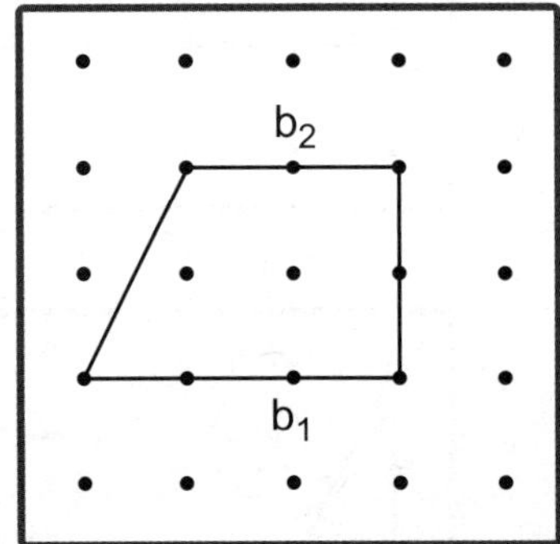

Area: ______________

Formula: ______________

6.

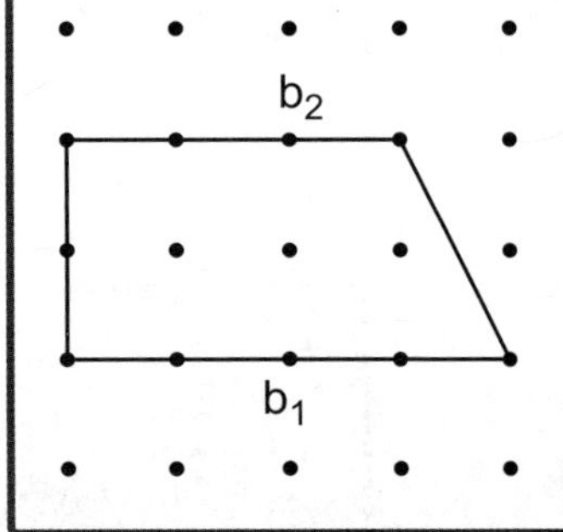

Area: ______________

Formula: ______________

Name: ______________________ Date: ______________________

Do You See a Pattern?

Look closely at the sets of 3 triangles, 3 squares, and 3 pentagons below. (Each set has something in common, but each shape in the set has a different area.) Then answer the questions that follow.

Set A

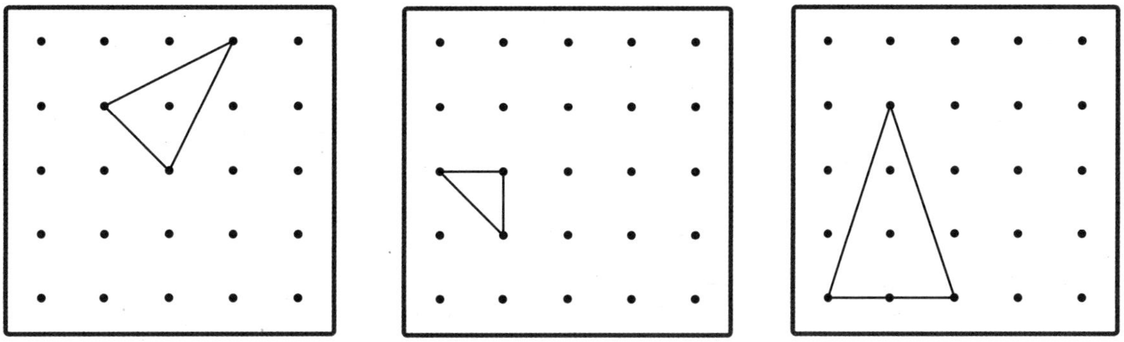

Set B

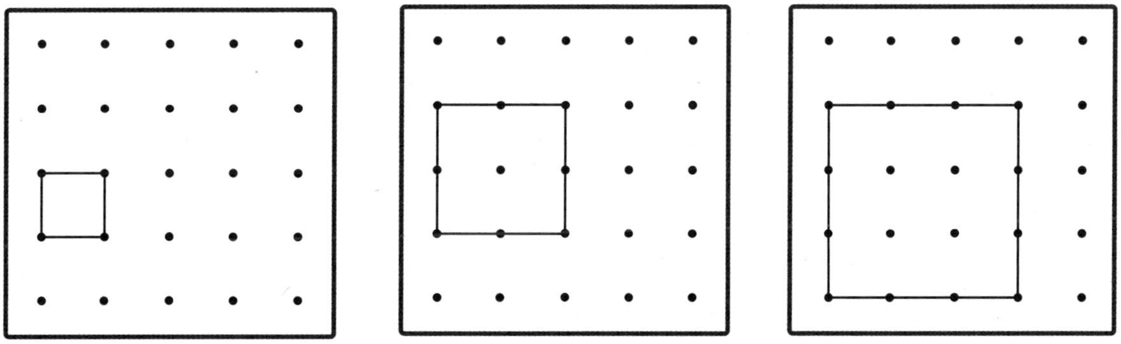

Set C

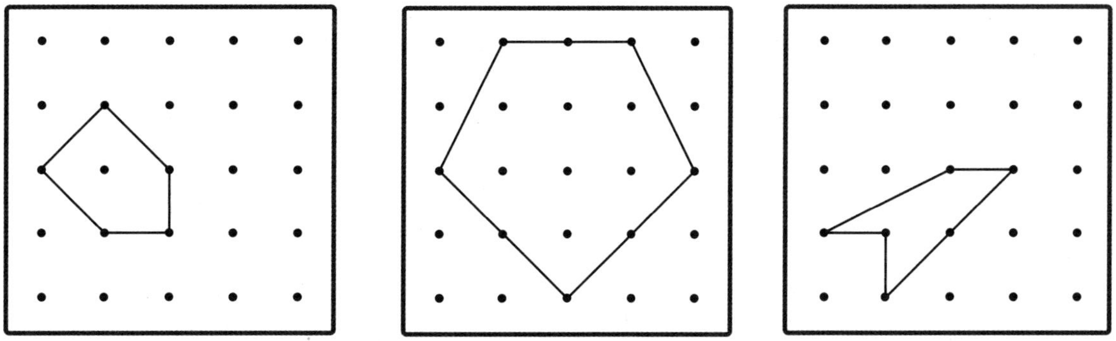

Name: ______________________ Date: ______________________

Do You See a Pattern? (cont.)

1. What do the three shapes in Set A have in common? How are they different?

2. What do the three shapes in Set B have in common? How are they different?

3. What do the three shapes in Set C have in common? How are they different?

4. Can you draw any general conclusions? Do you see a pattern?

PRACTICE

Name: ______________________ Date: ______________________

How Many Pins?

Below are three sets of exercises that will show you a new way to find areas on the geoboard. Each set asks you to make a shape with a specific number of pins inside the shape. For each shape you make, record the area and number of pins touched by the rubber band that forms the shape. A wonderful pattern exists. See whether you can discover it!

1. Make as many shapes as you can with **NO pins inside the shape.** Record your results in the table.

Area (A)	Number of Pins Touched by Rubber Band (N)	Number of Pins Inside the Shape (I)
		0
		0
		0
		0
		0

2. Make as many shapes as you can with **only 1 pin inside the shape.** Record your results in the table.

Area (A)	Number of Pins Touched by Rubber Band (N)	Number of Pins Inside the Shape (I)
		1
		1
		1
		1
		1

Name: ______________________ Date: ______________________

How Many Pins? (cont.)

3. Make as many shapes as you can with **just 2 pins inside the shape.** Record your results in the table.

Area (A)	Number of Pins Touched by Rubber Band (N)	Number of Pins Inside the Shape (I)
		2
		2
		2
		2
		2

4. What patterns did you discover? ______________________

____

____

____

____

5. Write the formula that describes the pattern. ______________________

3.2 Right Triangles and the Pythagorean Theorem

Main Ideas

Right triangles are special cases and, as such, are labeled as shown below:

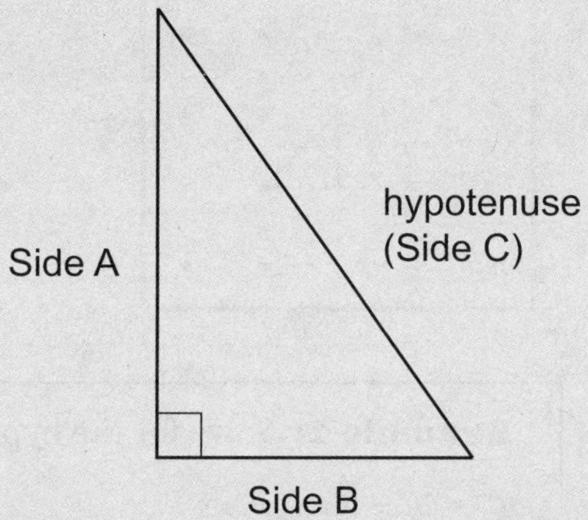

The side opposite the right angle in a right triangle is called the *hypotenuse.*

Every right triangle has the property that **the square of the hypotenuse is equal to the sum of the squares of the other two sides.** This property is known as the *Pythagorean Theorem.*

The Pythagorean Theorem is written as $a^2 + b^2 = c^2$. It can be used to find the length of one side of a right triangle if the lengths of the other two sides are known.

In the following activity, students use their geoboards to determine the length of the hypotenuse for the right triangle shown and then solve problems based on their new understanding of the Pythagorean Theorem.

If students need to construct bigger triangles to reinforce understanding of the Pythagorean Theorem, have them use a 121-pin geoboard.

PRACTICE

Name: ____________________ Date: ____________________

Right Triangles and the Pythagorean Theorem

Make the right triangle shown below, and make a square on each side as shown.

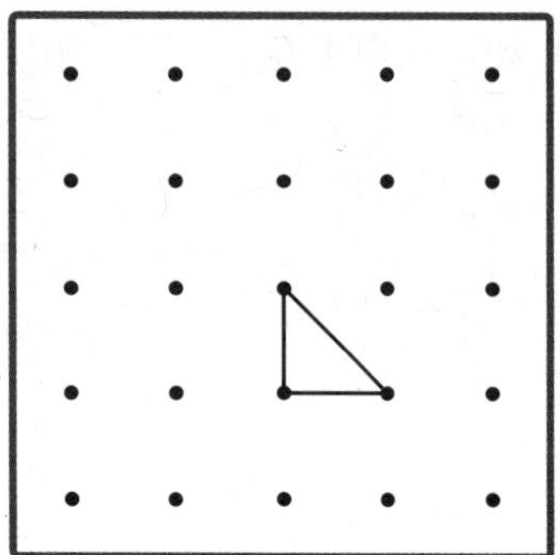

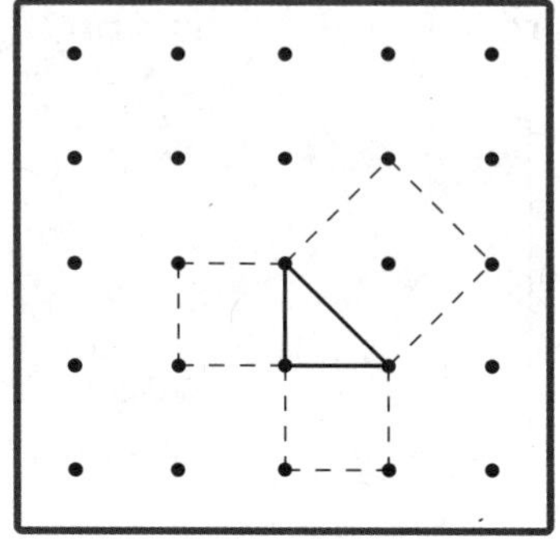

1. What do you notice? What is the length of the hypotenuse? Can you guess the formula for finding the hypotenuse?

____

____

____

____

____

Example 1: Solve for the hypotenuse.

$c^2 = a^2 + b^2$

$c^2 = (8)^2 + (6)^2$

$c^2 = 64 + 36$

$c^2 = 100$

$c = \sqrt{100}$

$c = 10$

c

6

8

The hypotenuse of the triangle is 10.

Example 2: Solve for the length of the missing leg of the triangle.

$a^2 + b^2 = c^2$

$(9)^2 + b^2 = (15)^2$

$81 + b^2 = 225$

$b^2 = 225 - 81$

$b^2 = 144$

$b = \sqrt{144}$

$b = 12$

15

b

9

The length of the missing leg is 12.

Now use the Pythagorean Theorem to find the missing length of the triangles with the given dimensions below.

2. $a = 5$, $b = 12$, $c =$ __________

3. $a = 7$, $c = 25$, $b =$ __________

4. $a = 3$, $b = 4$, $c =$ __________

3.3 Formulas for Perimeter

Main Idea

Perimeter is the distance around a figure. For polygons, “distance around” means the sum of the lengths of the sides.

For some polygons, a simple formula will give us the perimeter. For other polygons, students will have to solve perimeter questions on their own.

Students may have already discovered the formula for the perimeter of a rectangle. If they haven’t, remind them that the opposite sides of a rectangle are equal, so the formula for the perimeter of a rectangle is $P = 2l + 2w$.

Name: ______________________ Date: ______________________

Polygon Perimeters

Find the perimeter (*P*) for each polygon shown below. For 7–9, first find the length of the hypotenuse.

1. 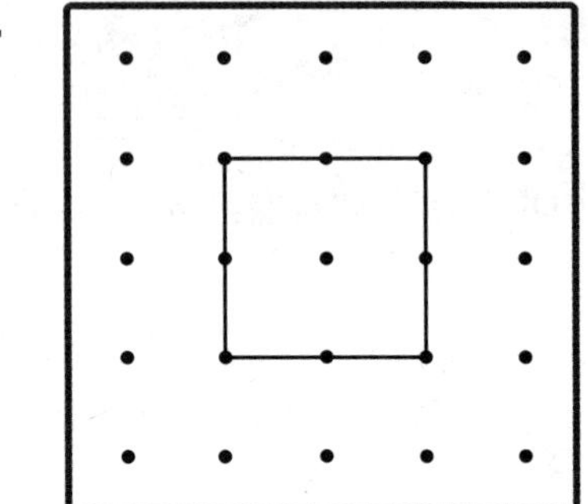

P = ______________

2. 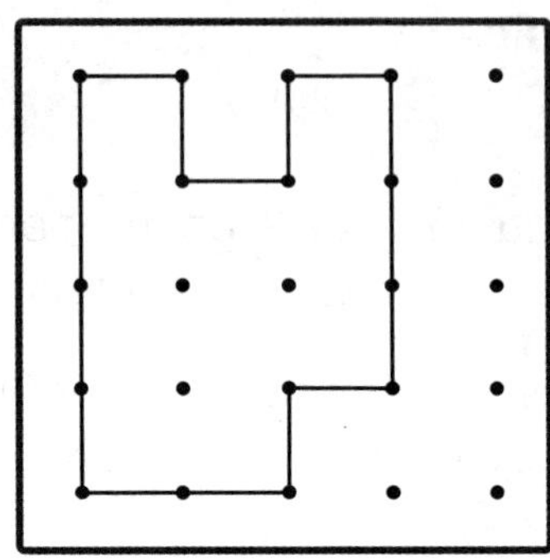

P = ______________

3. 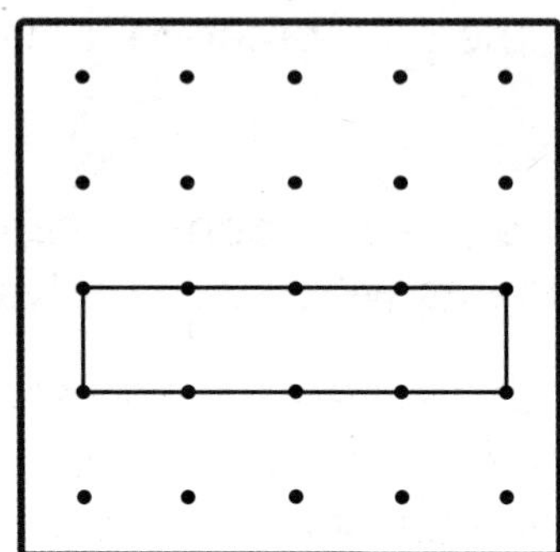

P = ______________

4. 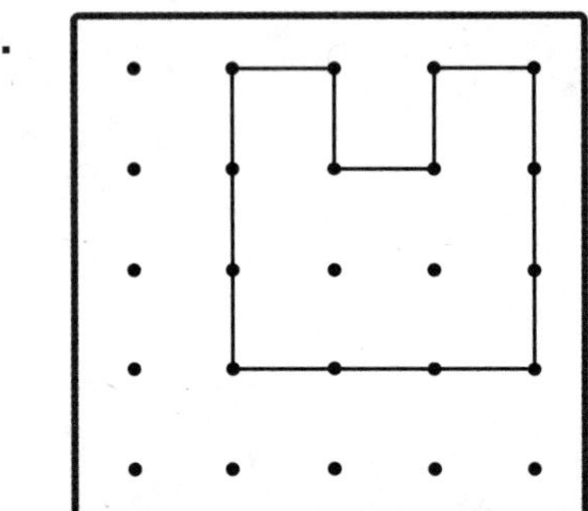

P = ______________

5. 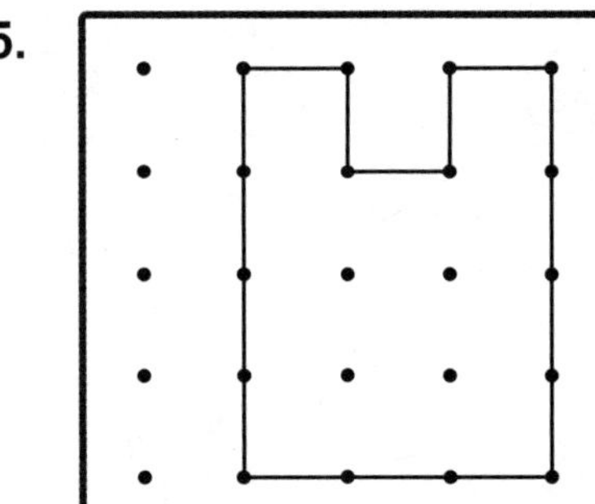

P = ______________

6. 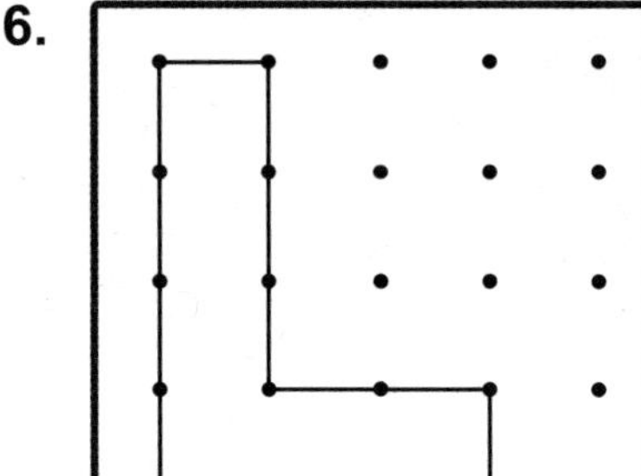

P = ______________

7. 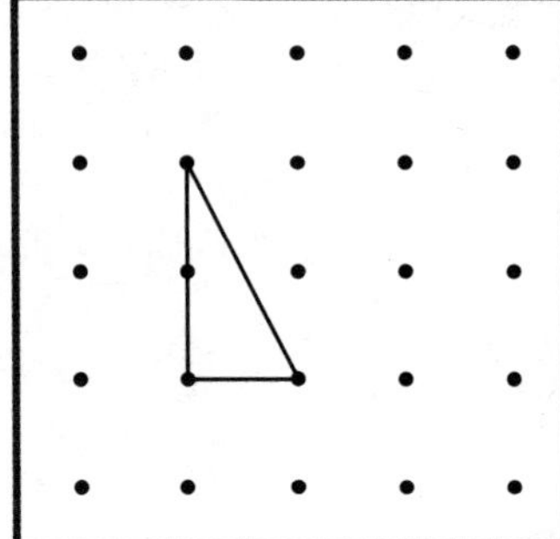

P = ______________

8. 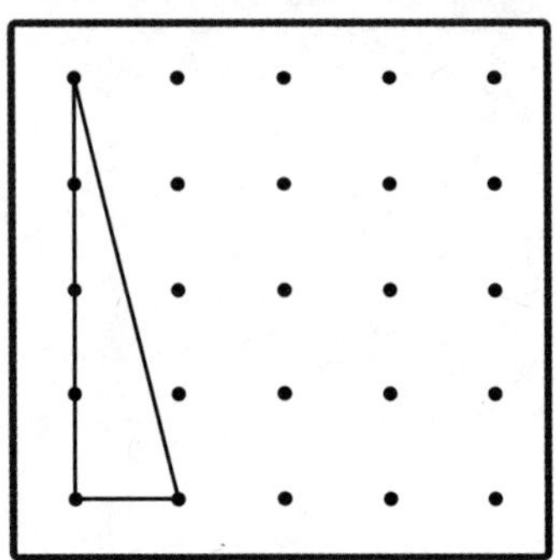

P = ______________

9. 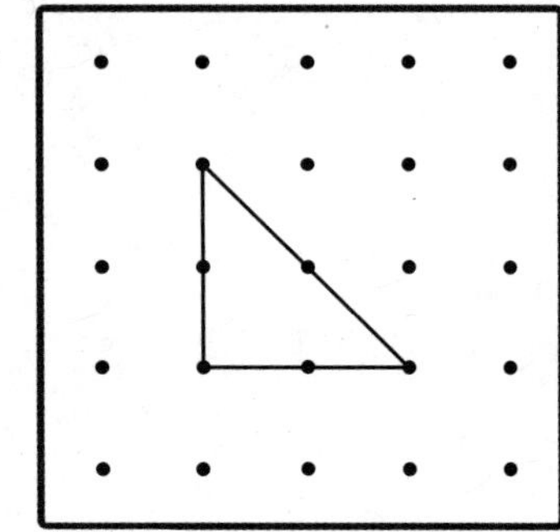

P = ______________

Name: ______________________ Date: ______________

Perimeter Word Problems

Using what you discovered about perimeters with your geoboard, solve the following problems.

Here is an example:

Find the perimeter of this rectangle.

$l = 60$ m

$w = 40$ m

Write the formula.	$P = 2l + 2w$
Substitute the data.	$P = (2 \times 60) + (2 \times 40)$
Solve the problem.	$P = 120 + 80$
	$P = 200$

The perimeter of the rectangle is 200 meters.

1. If you want to build a rectangular fence around your garden that is 12 ft. wide and 10 ft. long, how much fencing will you need?

____

2. A rectangular picture measures 39 centimeters by 50 centimeters. How much trim is needed to go around the picture?

____

PRACTICE

Name: ______________________ Date: ______________________

The Same but Different

In the shapes shown below, notice that the area (*A*) remains the same but the perimeter (*P*) changes.

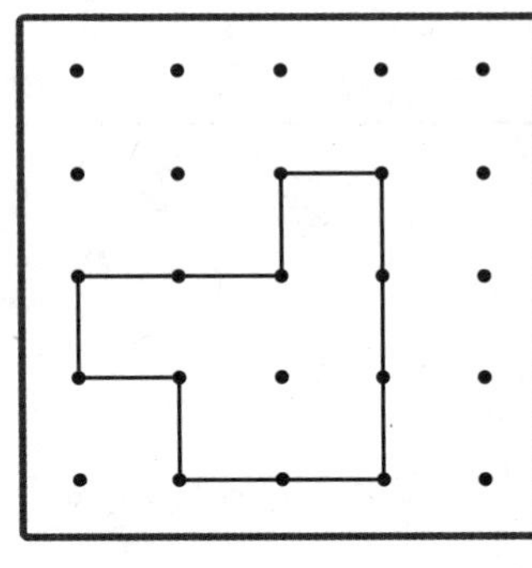

A = 6; *P* = 12

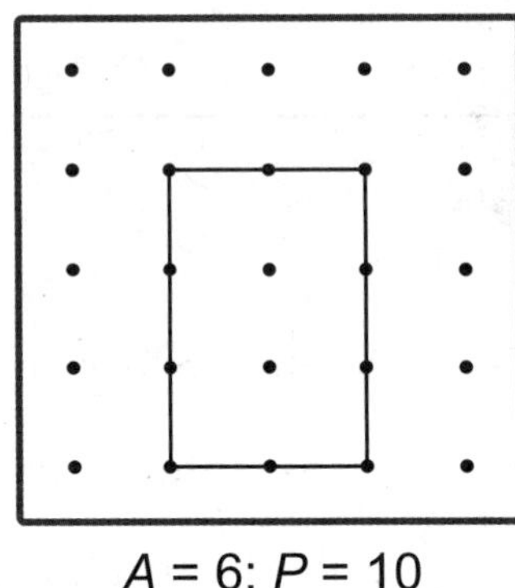

A = 6; *P* = 10

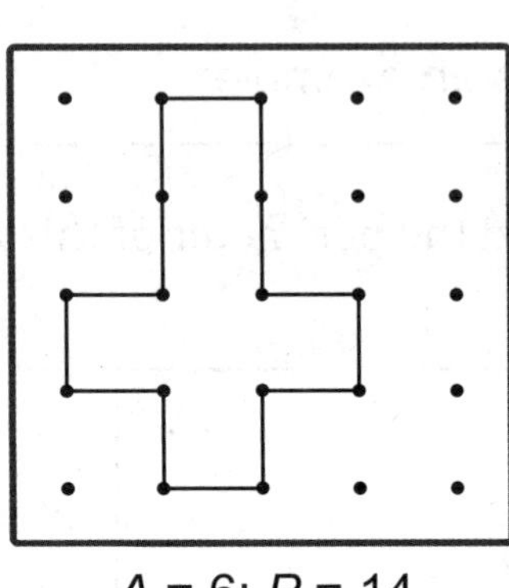

A = 6; *P* = 14

Make some shapes on your geoboard and see whether the perimeter always changes when the shape is different but the area is the same. Sketch your findings on the blank geoboards below. No right triangles allowed!

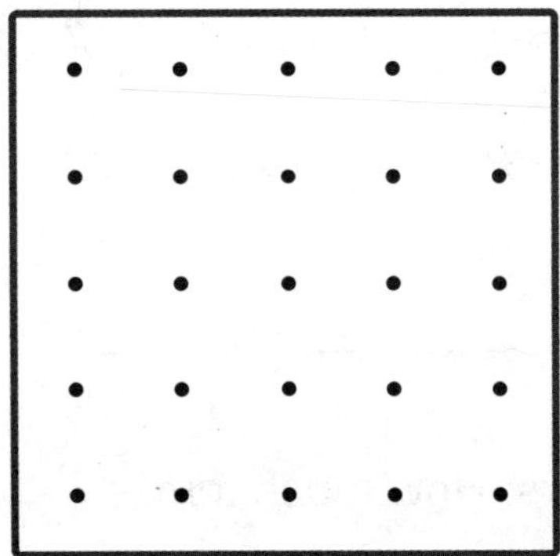

A = ________ *P* = ________

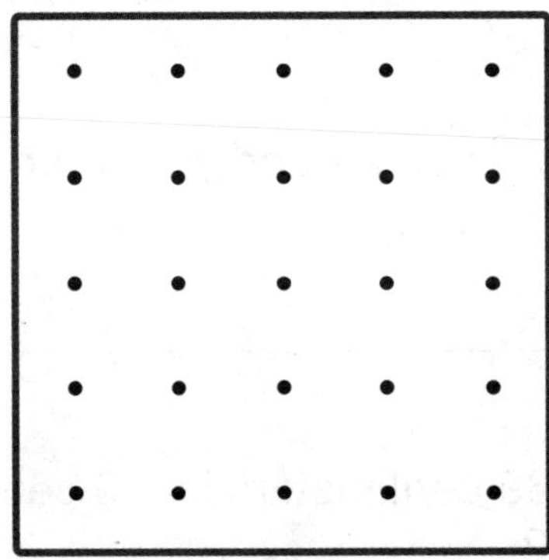

A = ________ *P* = ________

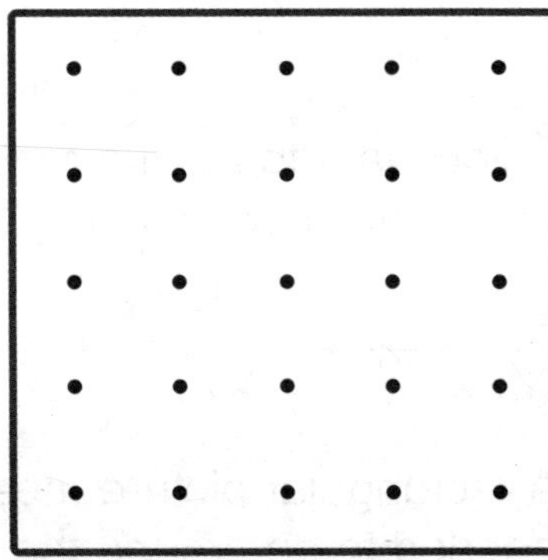

A = ________ *P* = ________

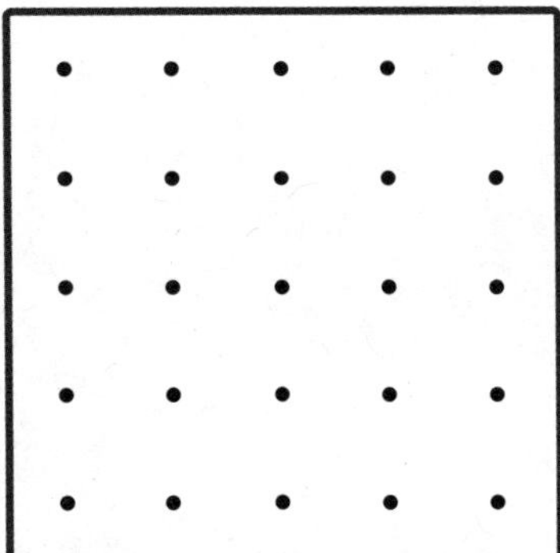

A = ________ *P* = ________

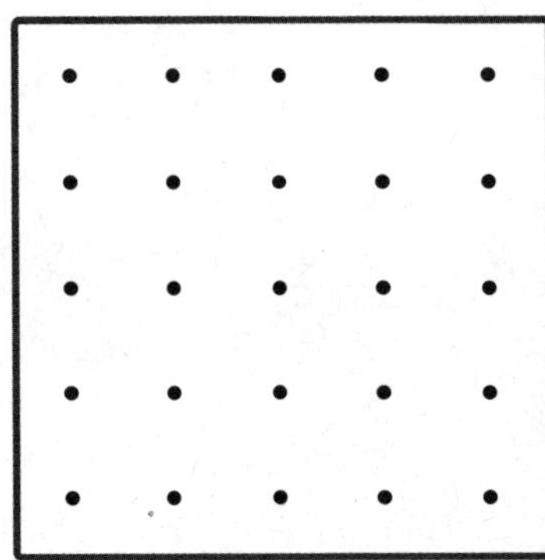

A = ________ *P* = ________

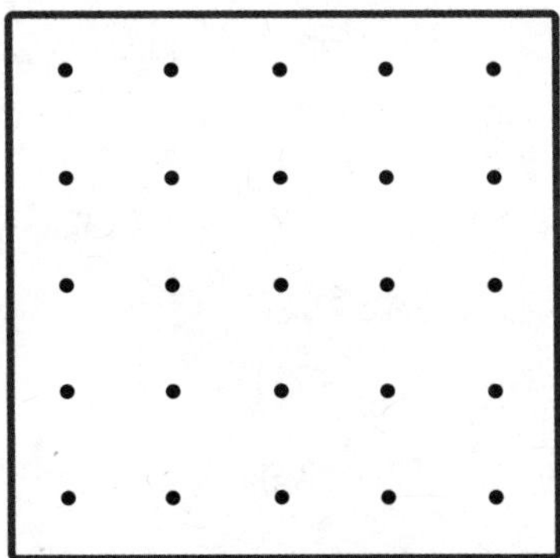

A = ________ *P* = ________

Name: ________________________ Date: ________________________

Area and Perimeter

Use your geoboard to answer the following questions. Sketch the shapes you make.

1. How many different-sized squares can you make on your geoboard? __________

2. Can you make a rectangle on your geoboard with an area of 6 square units? ______

3. Can you make squares on your geoboard with areas of 1, 2, 3, 4, 5, 6, 7, 8, and 9?

   ____

4. Can you make at least 3 different quadrilaterals on your geoboard that have an area of 8 square units? ________________________

5. Can you make a square that has an area equal to the perimeter? __________

6. Can you make 3 different shapes with perimeters of 12 units? __________

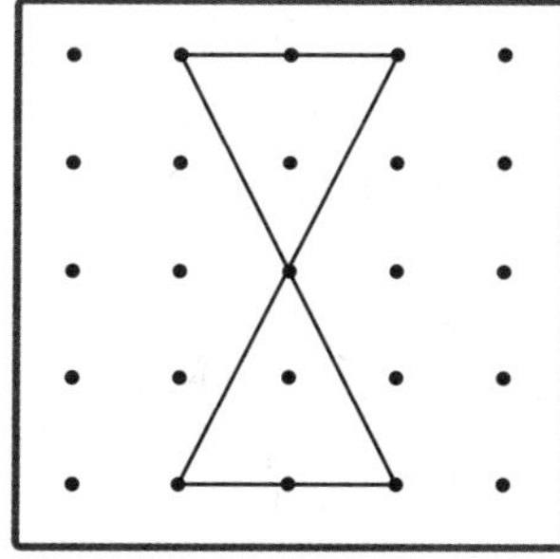

Figure 1

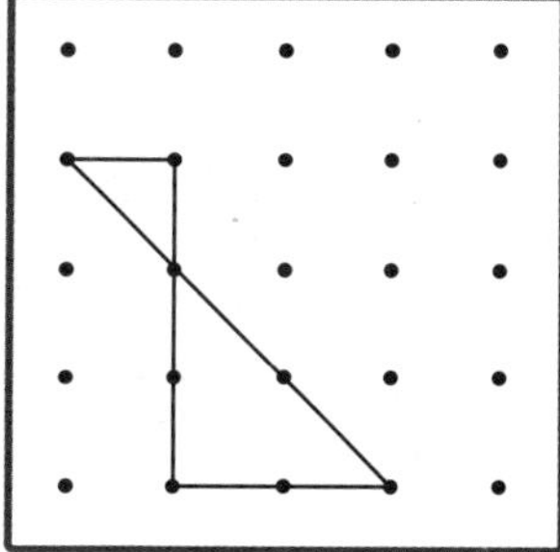

Figure 2

7. Look at Figure 1. How do the areas of the two triangles compare? __________
   How do their perimeters compare? ________________________

8. Look at Figure 2. How does the area of the larger triangle compare with the area of the smaller triangle? ________________________

   ____

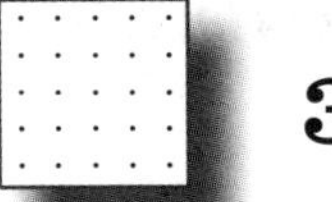

3.4 Patterns

Main Idea

Many sequences have patterns that can be discovered by careful study. For example, the number sequence 2, 4, 6, 8, 10, 12, …, has the pattern $B = 2A$.

A is the position of the number in the sequence (1, 2, 3, 4, 5, 6, …) and B is the number in the sequence (2, 4, 6, 8, 10, 12…):

Position (A)	1	2	3	4	5	6	7
Number (B)	2	4	6	8	10	12	14

Here is another example: The numbers in the pattern (B) are 2, 6, 12, 20, 30, 42, …, and A is the position of the number in the sequence (1, 2, 3, 4, 5, 6, …).

Position (A)	1	2	3	4	5	6	7
Number (B)	2	6	12	20	30	42	56

The pattern equation is $B = A(A + 1)$.

In the following activities, students use their geoboards to study the relationship between the area of a square and its side length and the relationship between the number of sides of a given polygon (square, pentagon, and so on) and the number of diagonals that shape has.

Before students do the diagonals activity (page 40), discuss the definition of a *diagonal* as *a line that connects nonadjacent (not next to each other) vertices of a polygon* and demonstrate as necessary.

Note that for the triangles activity (page 41), students will *not* be able to make all the triangles on their geoboards as shown, but they should have a good idea of how to complete the activity based on their experiences working with patterns in the squares and diagonals activities preceding it.

PRACTICE

Name: ______________________ Date: ______________

Counting Up Squares

Study these shapes and look for a pattern. Then complete the following table to see whether you can find a relationship between the squares in the sequence and the lengths of the sides of the squares. Then write the formula. Let *L* represent the length of a side and *N* the number of squares enclosed by the figure (the area).

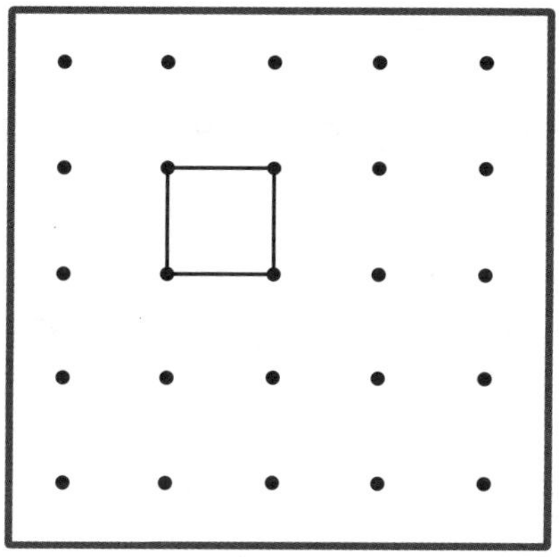

Figure 1

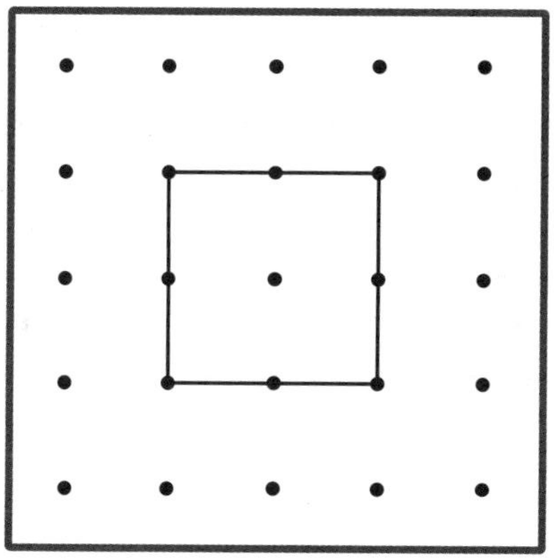

Figure 2

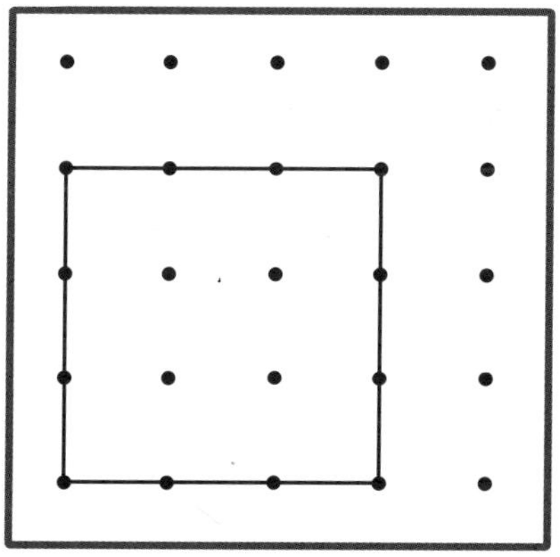

Figure 3

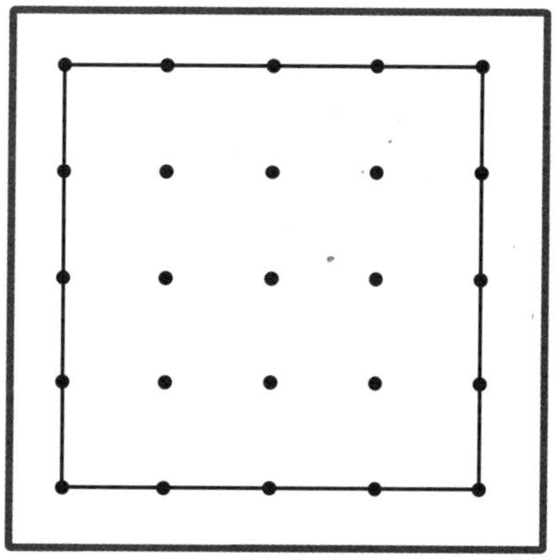

Figure 4

***L* (length of side)**	1	2	3	4	5	6	7	8
***N* (number of squares)**								

The formula is ______________________.

Name: ______________________ Date: ______________

Counting Up Diagonals

Recall that a *diagonal* is a line that connects nonadjacent (not next to each other) vertices of a polygon.

Make each of the following shapes on your geoboard. Use rubber bands to show the diagonals and record the results in the table below. (The first one has been done for you.)

Then record the formula. Let *S* represent the number of sides of a figure and *N* the number of diagonals.

Shape	*S* (number of sides)	*N* (number of diagonals)
Triangle	3	0
Square		
Pentagon		
Hexagon		
Other (your choice)		

The formula is ______________________.

Name: ______________________________ Date: ____________________

Counting Up Triangles

Study these shapes and look for a pattern. Fill in the first four squares in table that follows. After you have filled in the first four squares, you should be able to see the pattern. Then fill in the rest of the table. (Be sure to count the upside-down triangles, too!)

(Hint: You will not be able to make all these shapes on your geoboard, but use what you've learned about patterns to complete the activity.)

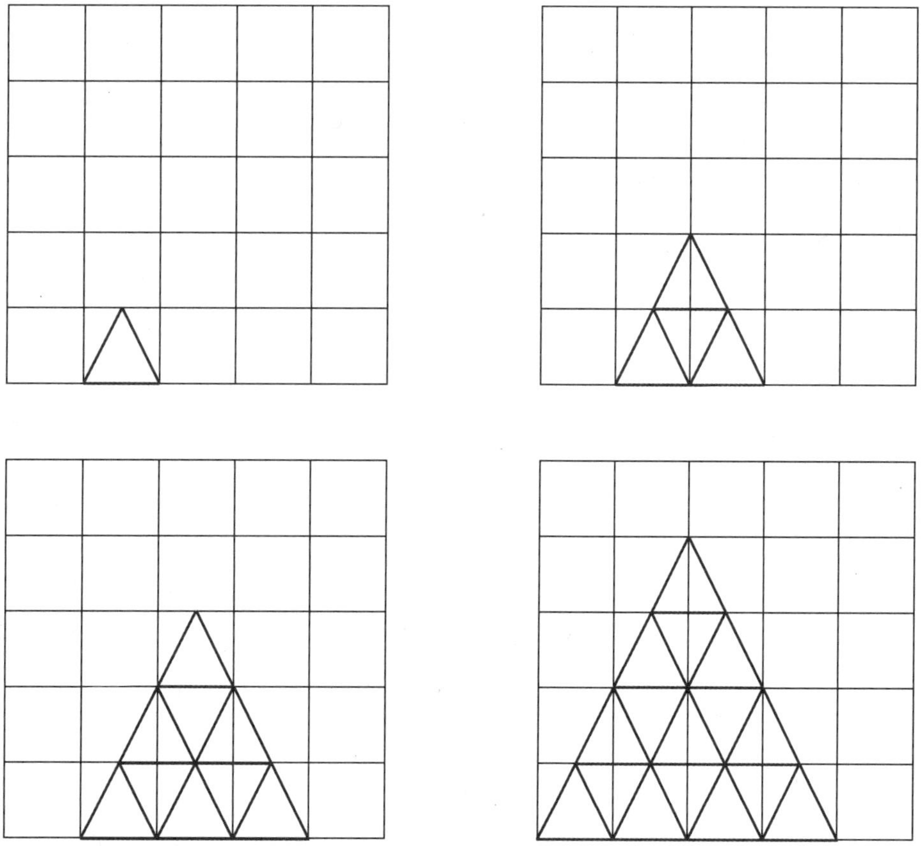

B **(length of base)**	1	2	3	4	5	6	7	8
T **(number of triangles)**								

Now write a formula based on your discovery. ______________________________

Chapter 4:
The Coordinate Plane on the Geoboard

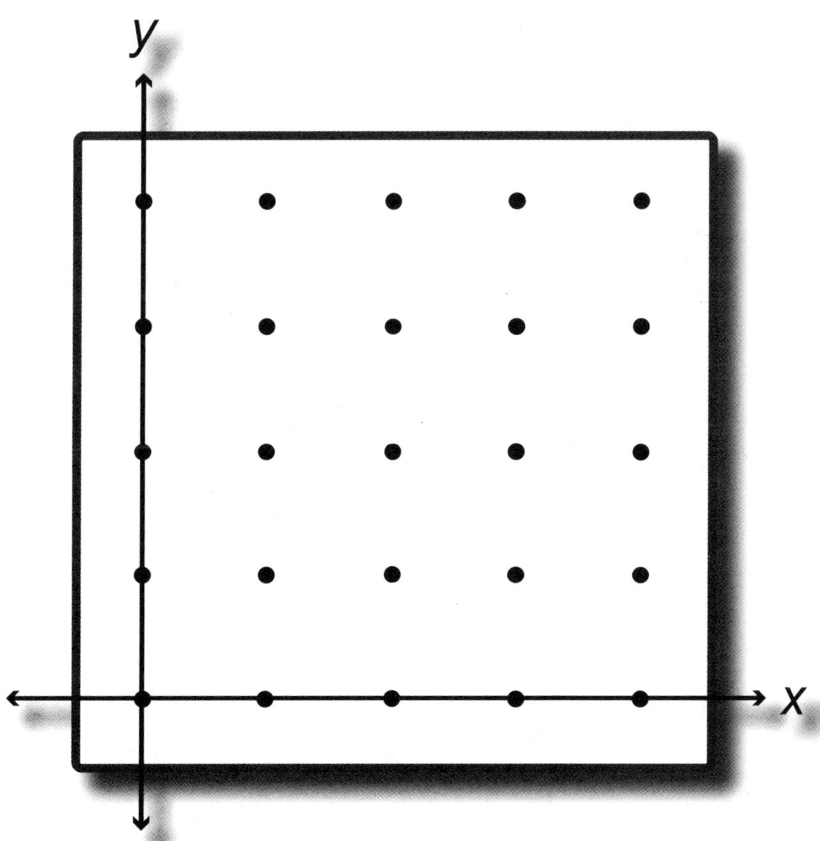

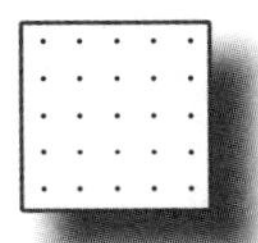

4.1 Points on the Coordinate Plane

Main Ideas

Any point on a coordinate plane can be identified by the two numbers representing it, called *coordinates*. As shown in the figures below, the coordinate plane is divided into four regions called *quadrants*, separated by the *x*-axis and *y*-axis and labeled as shown. These two axes are really two number lines, one horizontal and one vertical. The coordinates are written as ordered pairs (*x, y*) and the two coordinates are called the *abscissa* (*x*) and the *ordinate* (*y*).

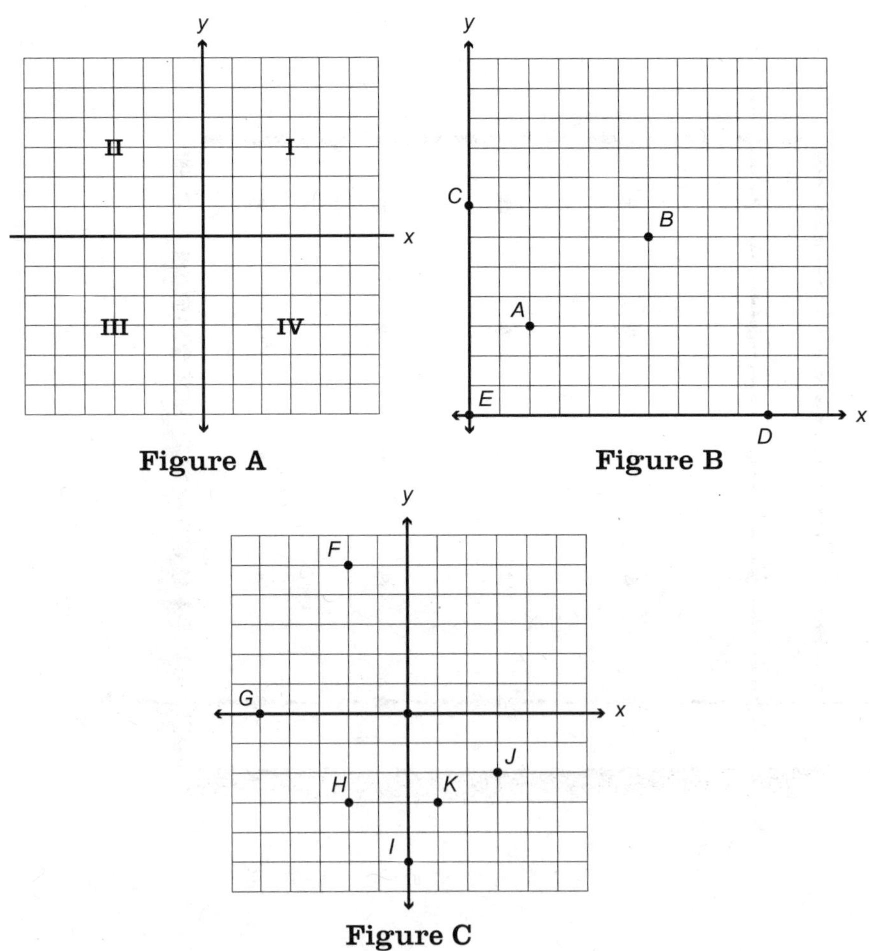

Figure A

Figure B

Figure C

Note that the coordinates for Figure *B* are *A*(2, 3); *B*(6, 6); *C*(0, 7); *D*(10, 0); and *E*(0, 0), and the coordinates for Figure *C* are *F*(⁻2, 5); *G*(⁻5, 0); *H*(⁻2, ⁻3); *I*(0, ⁻5); *J*(3, ⁻2); and *K*(1, ⁻3).

Students can practice locating points in the coordinate plane by playing Tic-Tac-Toe on the geoboard. Most students should be familiar with Tic-Tac-Toe, but if any are not, a practice game can be played in the first quadrant.

To play on the geoboard, it is necessary to use Unifix Cubes or chips with a hole in them to place on the pins. Use a different color for each player or team. The object of the game is to get FOUR markers of the same color in a row, horizontally, vertically, or diagonally.

Play a sample game with students on the geoboard in which the player or team represented by O goes first. Use this sequence of play:

O(2, 2), X(3, 2),

O(2, 1), X(2, 3),

O(3, 3), X(1, 4),

O(1, 1), X(4, 1).

Player or team X wins.

If necessary, replay this game with students until they understand the rules. Then play several more games with the students, making sure you play a game in each of the four quadrants.

Name: ______________________ Date: ______________________

Tic-Tac-Toe (first quadrant)

Play a game of Tic-Tac-Toe on your geoboard. Use the grid below to record your plays and their coordinates.

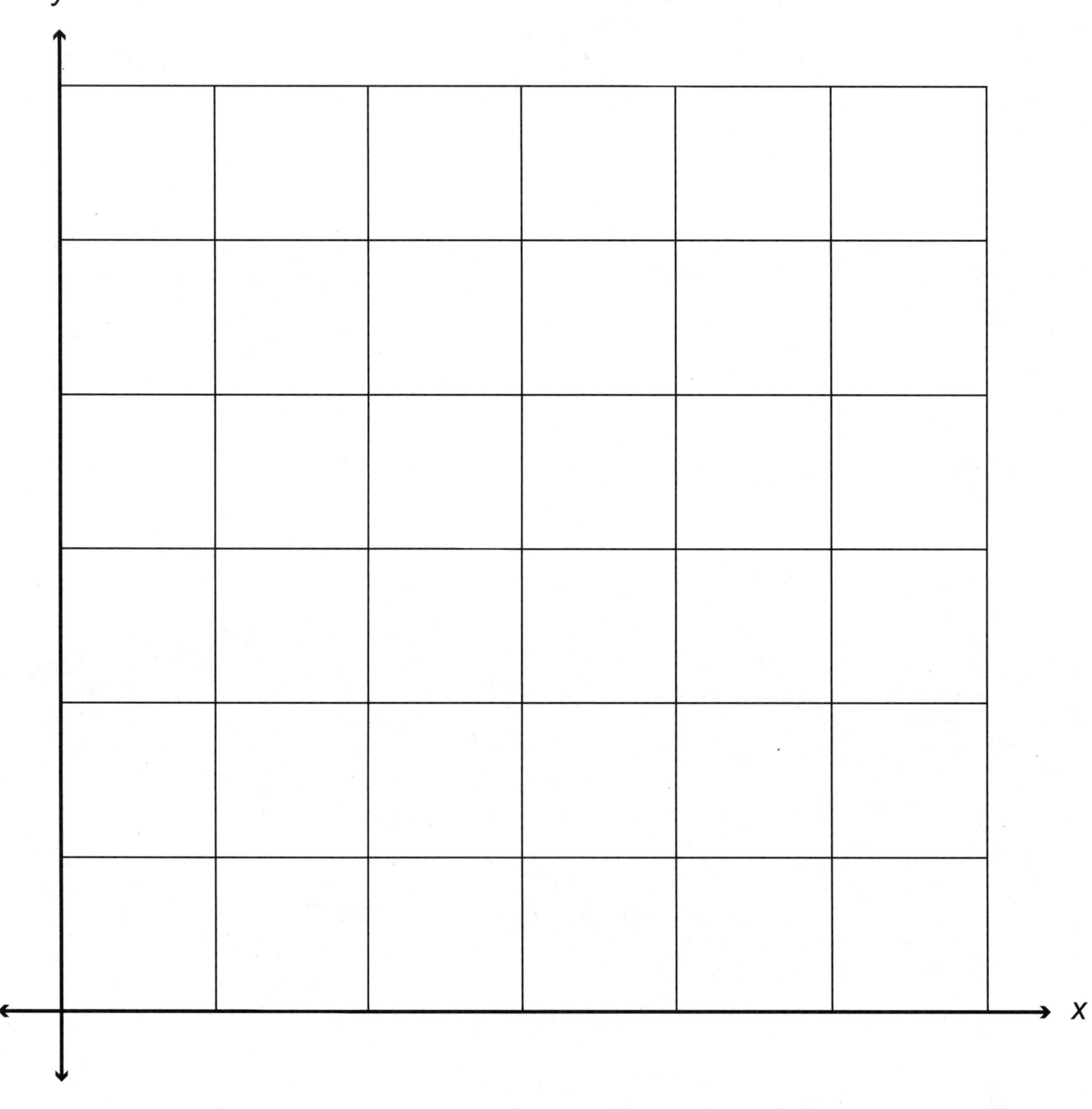

Name: ______________________ Date: ______________________

Tic-Tac-Toe (four quadrants)

Play a game of Tic-Tac-Toe on your geoboard. Use the grid below to record your plays and their coordinates.

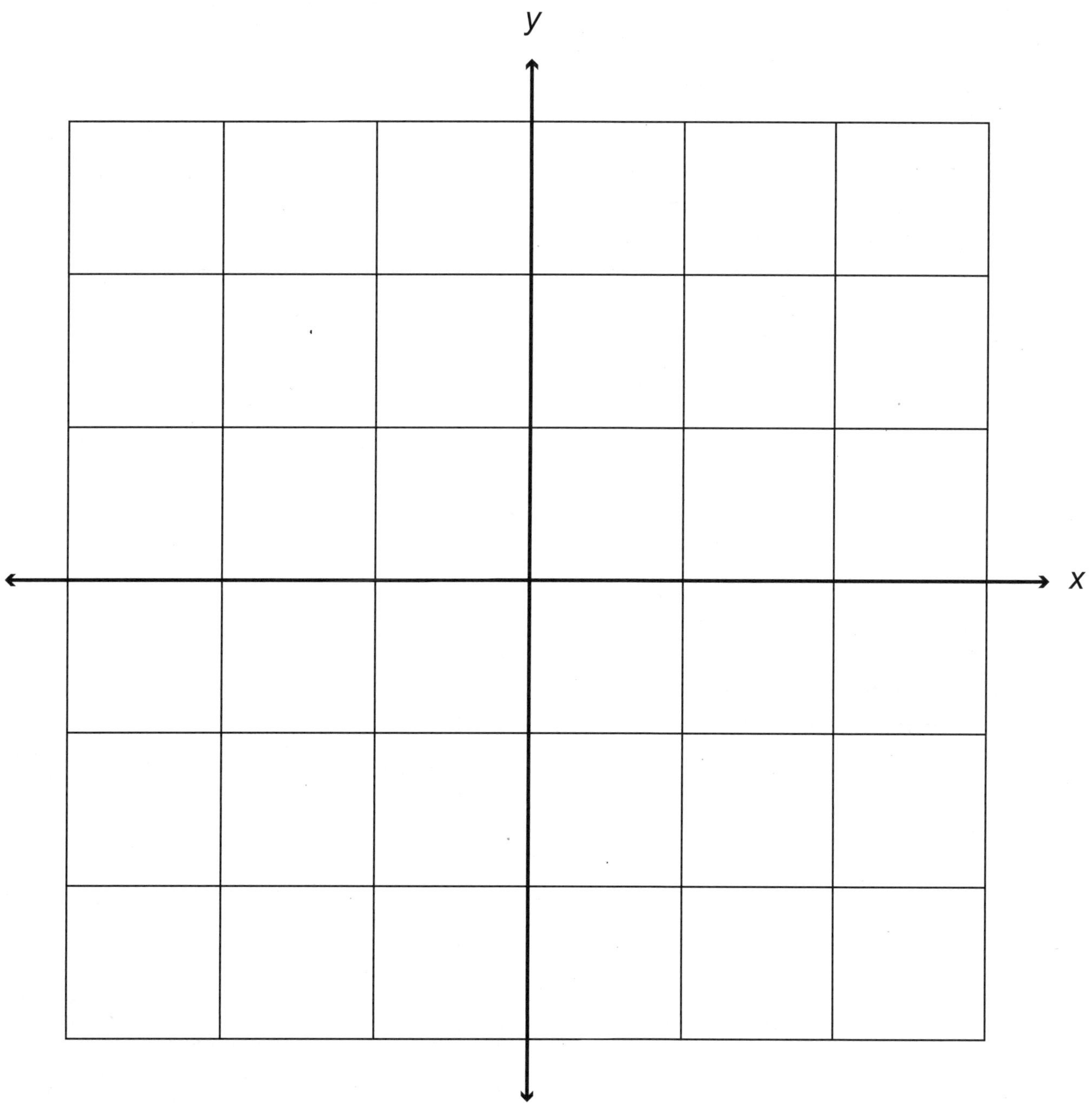

Name: ______________________ Date: ______________

Triangles on the Coordinate Plane

1. You have two pins, *A* and *B*, on your geoboard. *A* is located at the coordinate (1, 2) and *B* is at the coordinate (3, 2). Connect those two points with a rubber band. Suppose you wanted to connect the rubber band to a third point, *C*, to form a right triangle. How many right triangles could you make on your geoboard with *AB* as one of the sides?

   ______________ triangles

   (Sketch the triangles on the geoboard at right.)

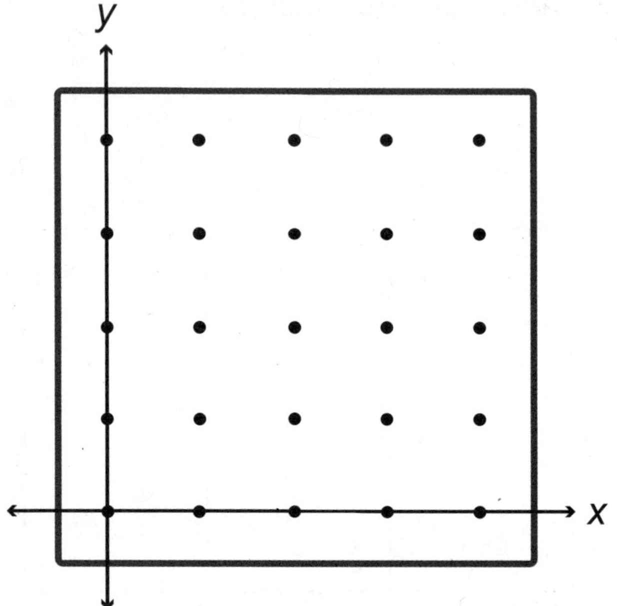

2. Suppose points *A* and *B* were located at coordinates (1,1) and (3, 2). How many right triangles could you make on your geoboard with *AB* as one side? Sketch them.

   ______________ triangles

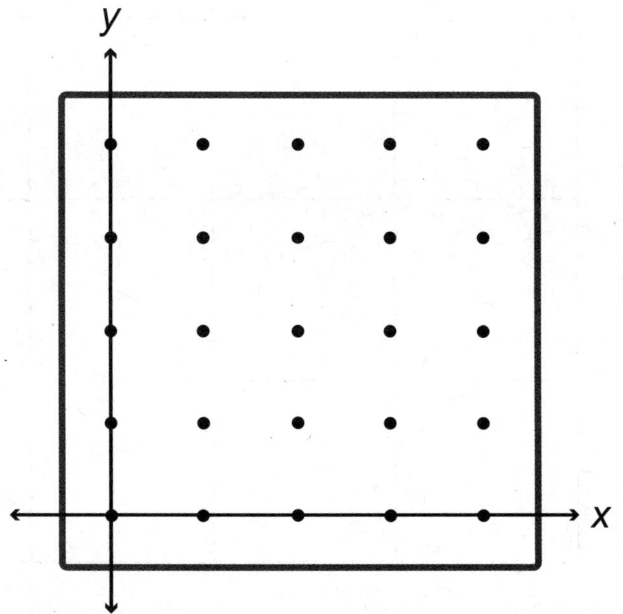

Chapter 5:
Shapes in Motion on the Geoboard

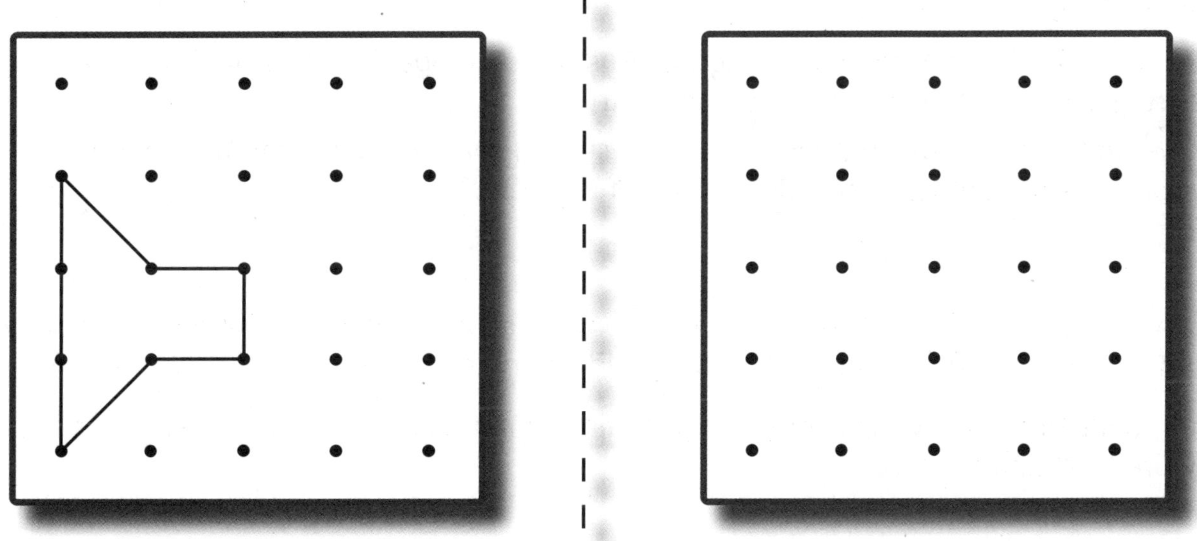

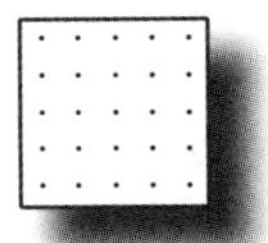

5.1 Rotations, Flips, and Symmetry

Main Ideas

There are three basic motion concepts that pertain to moving shapes in the coordinate plane: slides, flips, and rotations. Together, these three types of motions are called transformations.

Transformation – A movement of points in the coordinate plane that may change the shape, size, or position of a figure.

Slide – A transformation that moves a figure from one location to another on the coordinate plane without changing its size or shape.

Flip – A transformation that flips a figure over a set line in the coordinate plane, producing a mirror image.

Symmetry – The relationship of a figure to its mirror image. The line over which a figure is flipped is called the *line of symmetry.*

Rotation – A transformation that turns a figure in a given direction through an angle of rotation about a fixed point (the center of rotation).

Slides are so easy to do that they will not be considered here. Nothing changes except the location of the shape on the coordinate plane. Flips and rotations are different.

The first transformation we will consider is the flip. When you flip Figure 1 over the line, you get Figure 2, a mirror image.

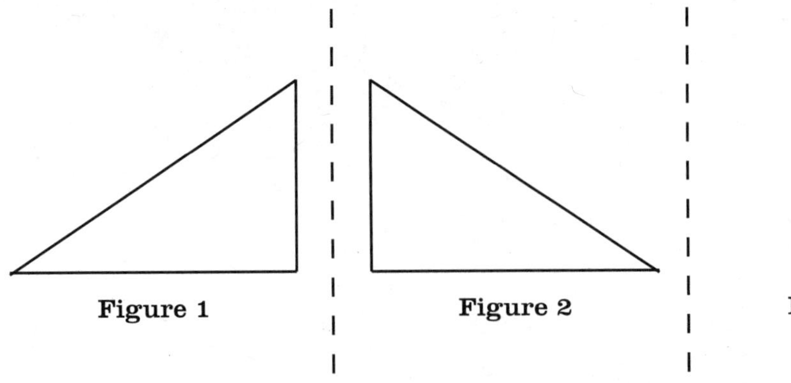

Have students make the next figure in the series on their geoboards by flipping Figure 2 over the given line to create Figure 3. Have them draw the resulting figure.

Next, have students look at rotations. It is easy to do 90-degree rotations of shapes constructed on the geoboard about a fixed point, provided the fixed point is located in a position that makes it possible for the shape to be rotated without going off the geoboard. The following pair of figures shows a 90-degree rotation of figure *ABCD* about a fixed point, E:

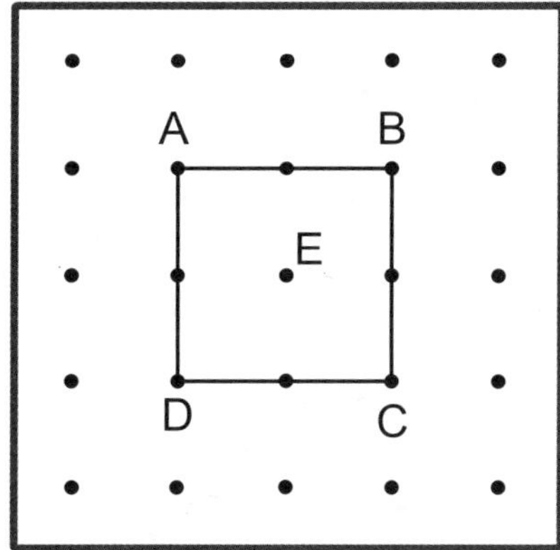

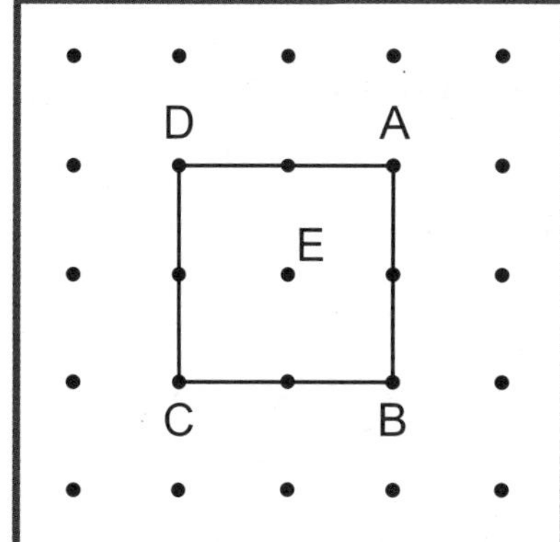

Have students do this rotation on their geoboards.

For other figures, flips and rotations may pose more of a challenge. Depending on their size and position, some figures may go "off" the physical geoboard when flipped or rotated, as in this example in which the square is rotated 90 degrees around point *C*.

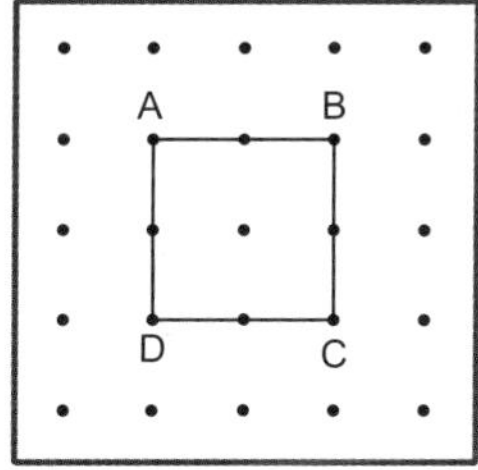

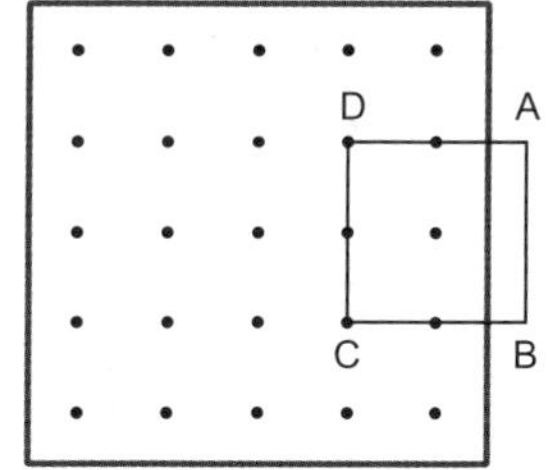

If students are having trouble visualizing flips or rotations for such figures, have them place two or four geoboards together to have a larger surface to work on:

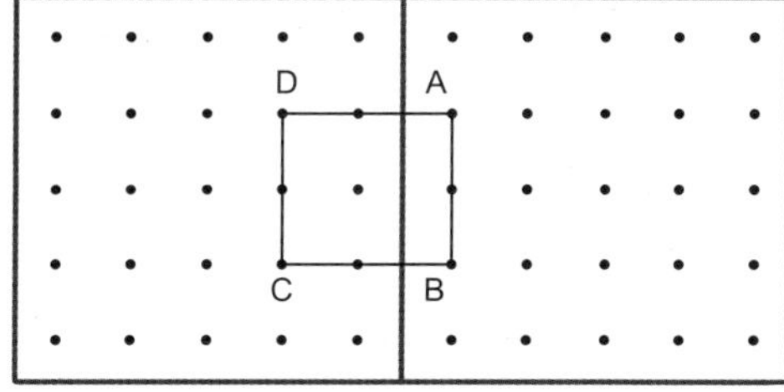

Or use a a 121-pin board.

Name: ______________________ Date: ______________________

Flips

Flip each figure on the left. Sketch the flipped figure on the blank geoboard on the right.

1.

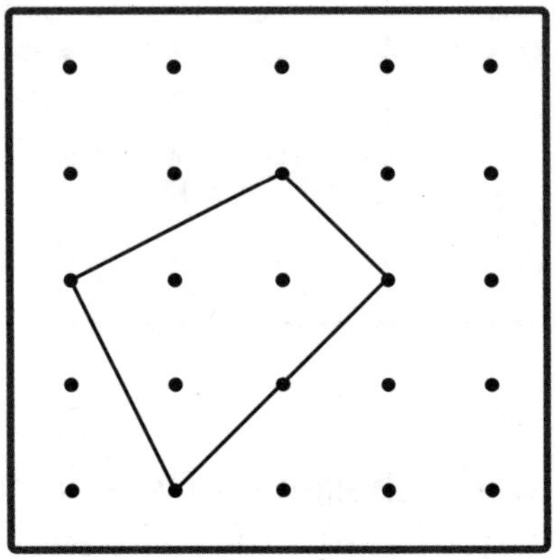

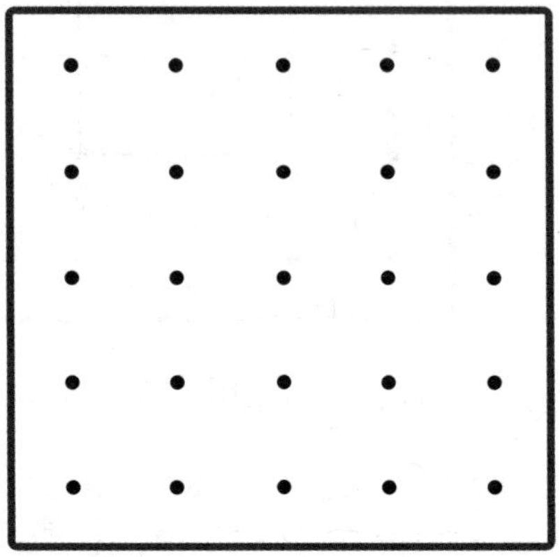

2.

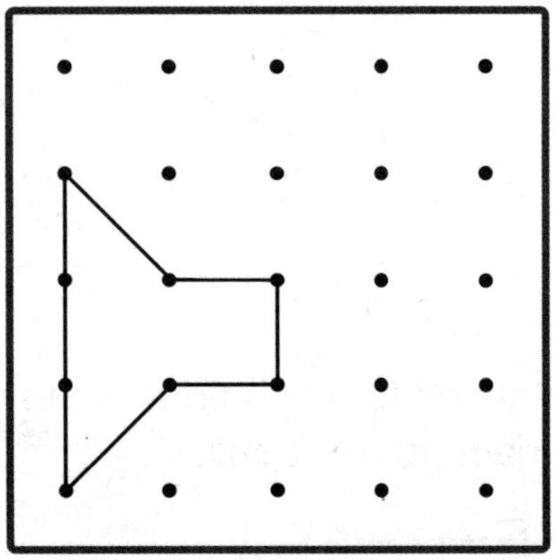

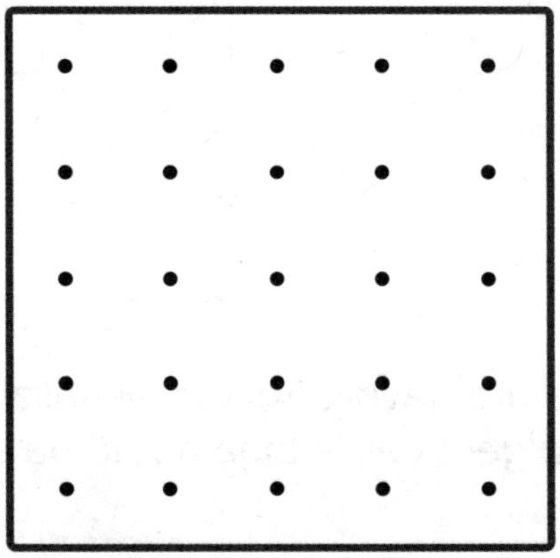

3.

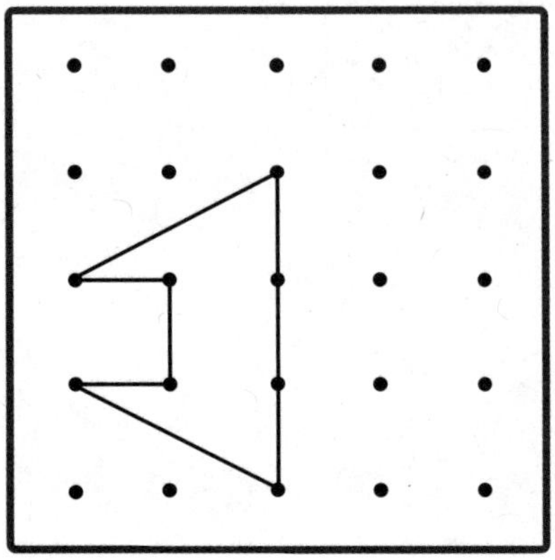

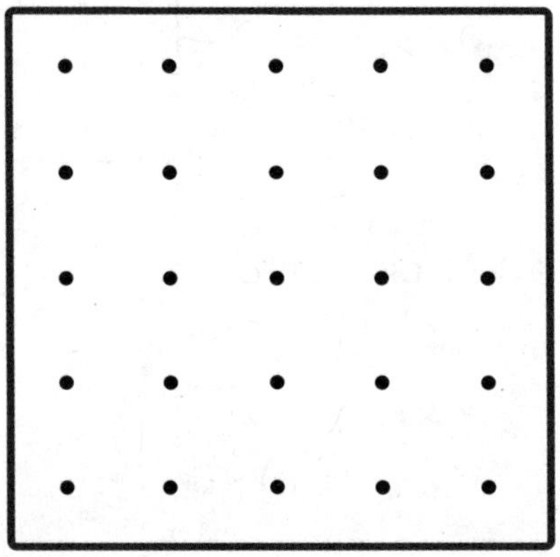

Name: ______________________ Date: ______________________

Rotations

1. Rotate figure *ABCD* 180 degrees clockwise about Point C. Sketch it on the blank geoboard on the right.

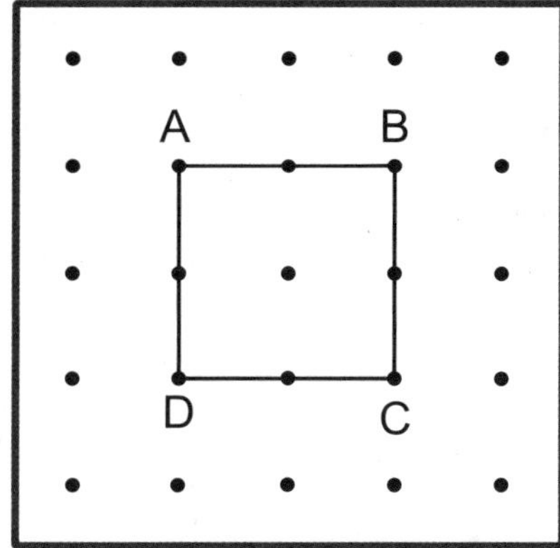

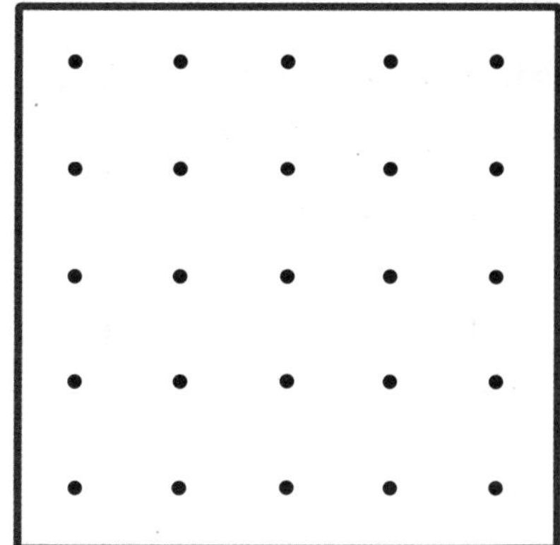

2. Rotate figure *ABCD* 270 degrees clockwise about Point C. Sketch it.

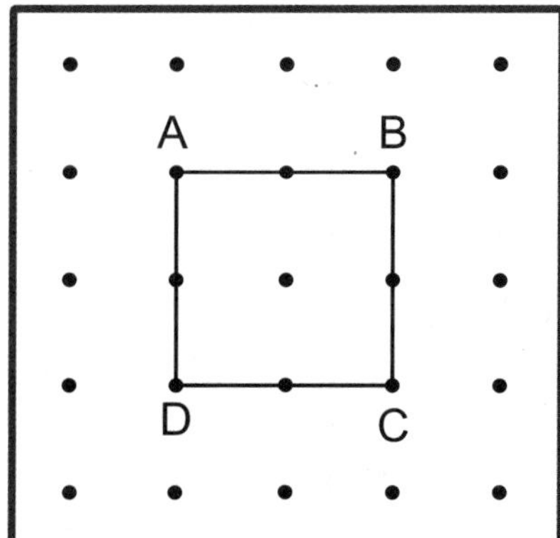

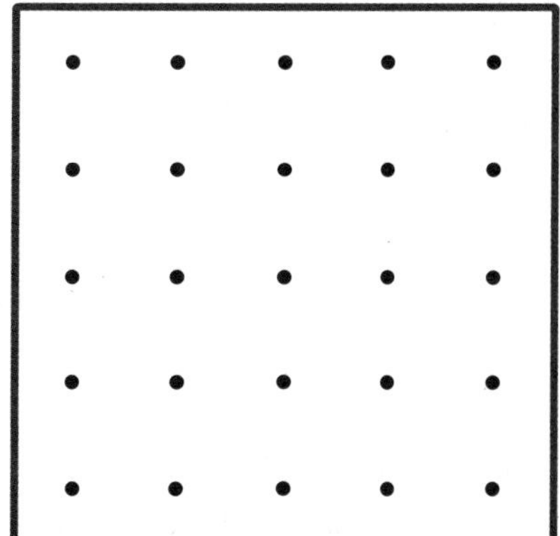

Name: ______________________ Date: ______________________

Flip and Rotate

Flip each figure on the left over line *l* and sketch the new figure in column B.

Then rotate each figure clockwise 90 degrees about point A. (Hint: Turn your geoboard to see the new position.)

Sketch the rotated figure in column C.

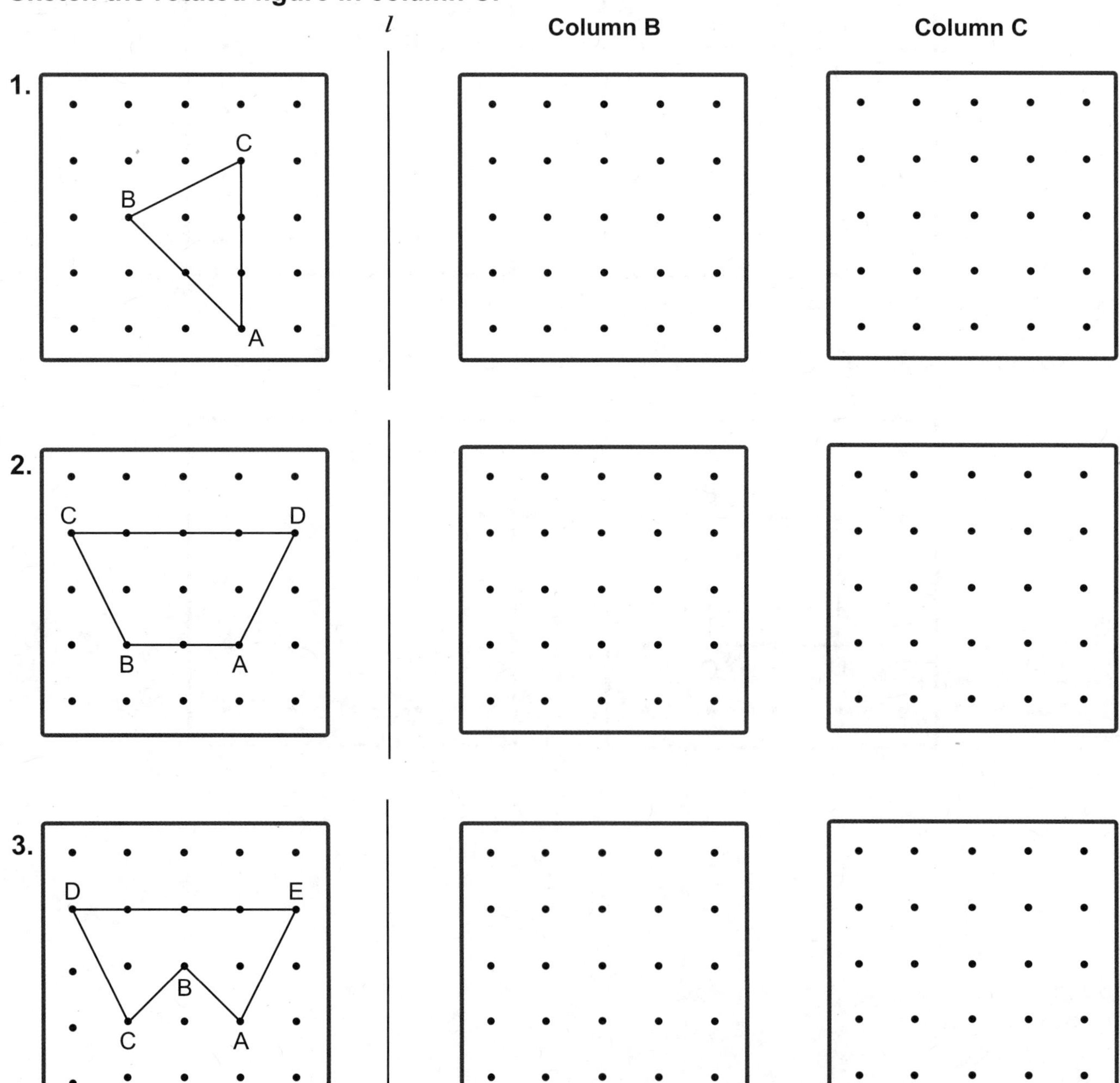

Name: ______________________ Date: ______________________

Symmetry

Recall that symmetry is the relationship of a figure to the mirror image of the figure about a given line, called the *line of symmetry.*

Show the symmetrical image for each of the following. Note the line of symmetry is given by line *l*. If you have difficulty, use a mirror.

1.

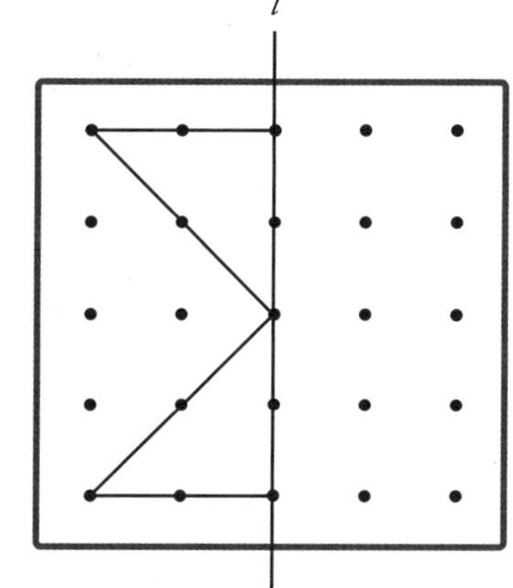

2.

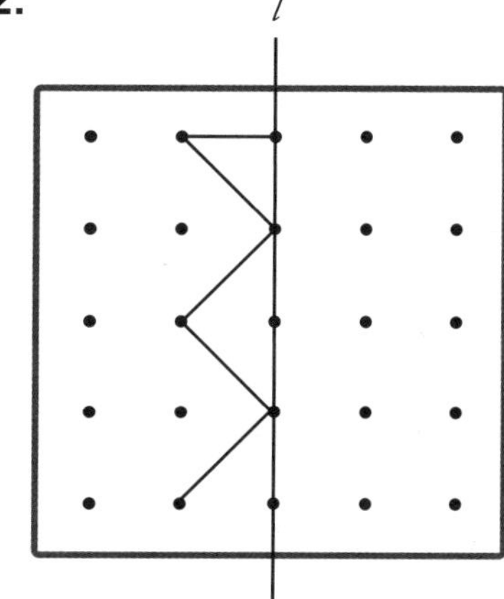

3.

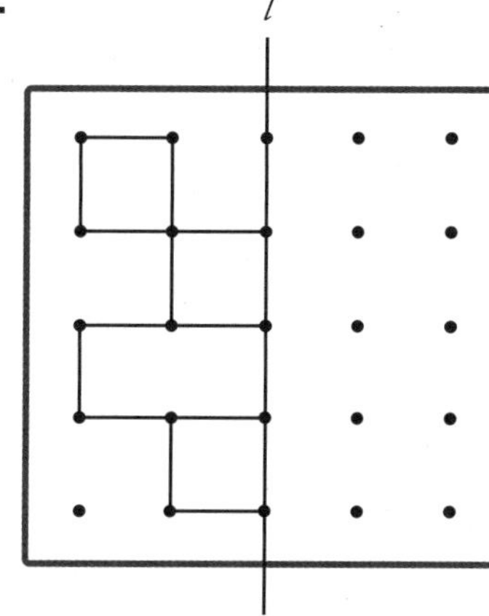

4.

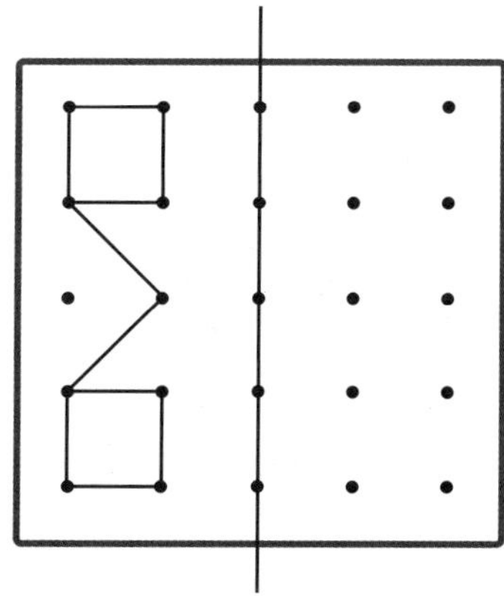

5.

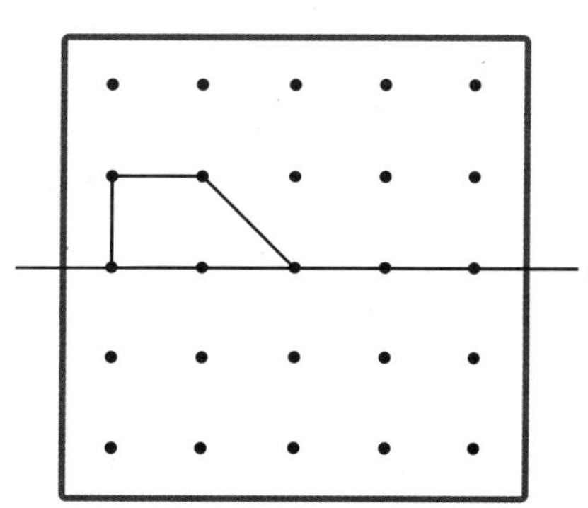

6.

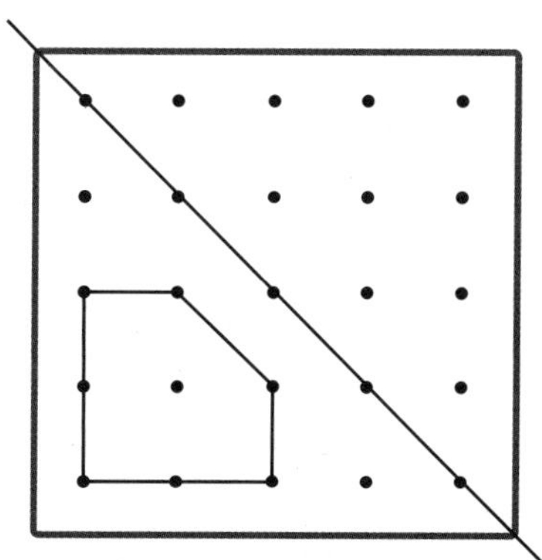

Name: ____________________ Date: ____________________

Shapes in Motion

Circle the correct answers.

1. Figure 2, the mirror image of Figure 1, looks the same as it would if it were rotated 360 degrees about point B.

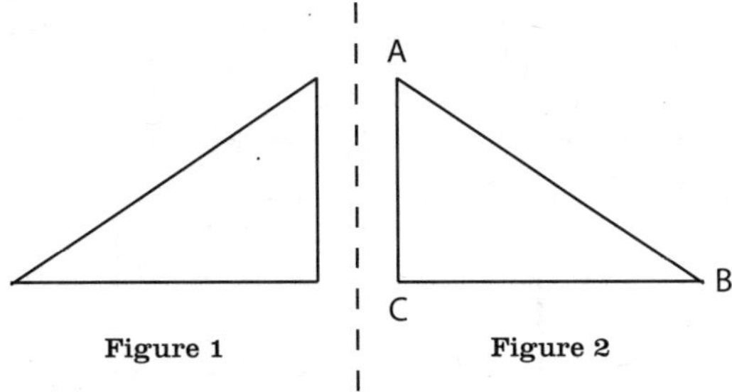

True **False**

2. When flipping a figure over a line, *l*, the points closest to the line *l* are farthest from the line *l* after the figure is flipped.

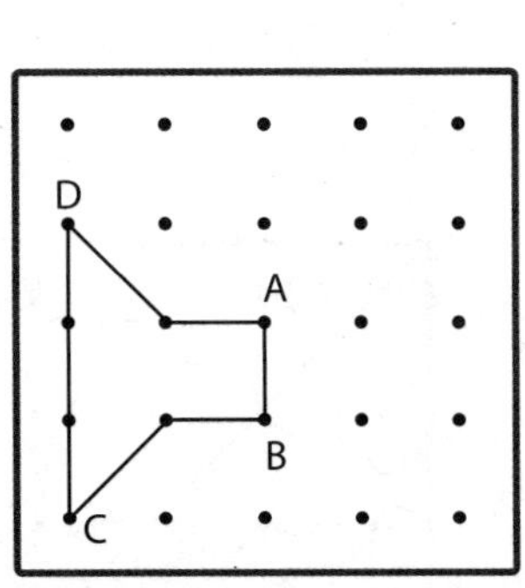

l

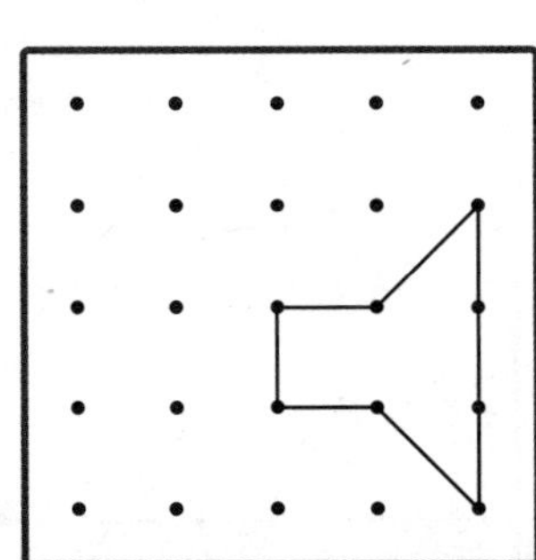

True **False**

3. Look back at the exercises on page 54. Would you get the same results in Column C if you rotated each shape first and then flipped it?

Yes **No**

Chapter 6:

Slope on the Geoboard

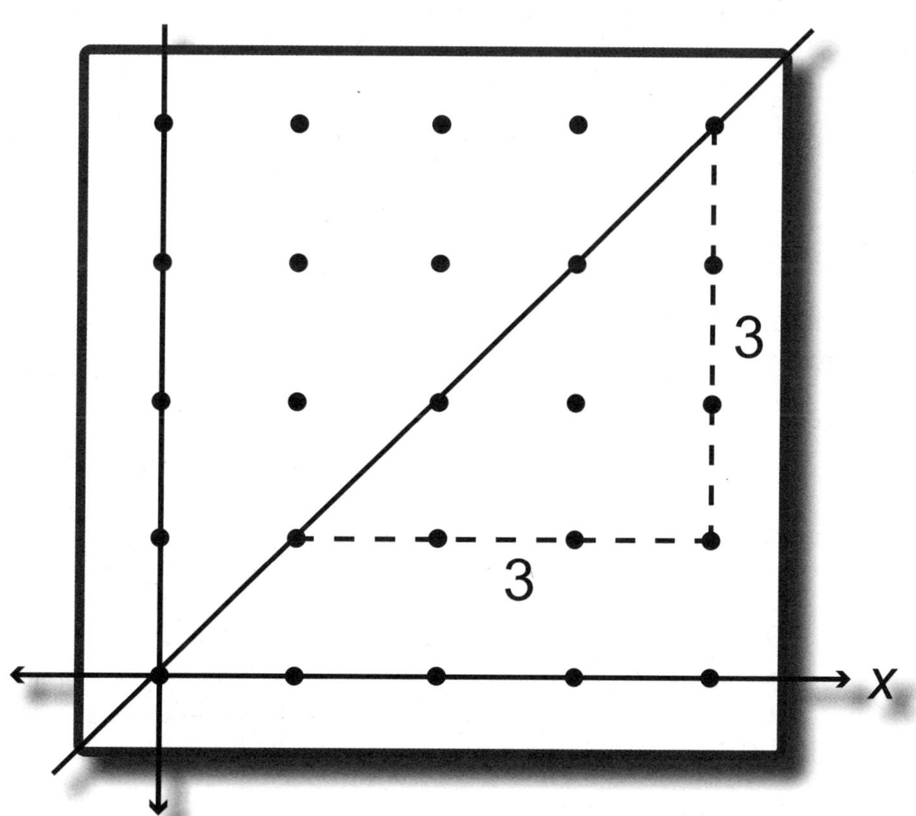

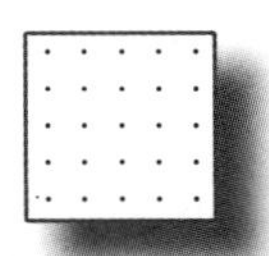

6.1 Slope and the Names of Lines

Main Ideas

Two points determine a line. A *line* is defined as a set of points that extends without end in opposite directions.

The *slope* of a line is determined by any two points on the line. The slope of a line tells how steep the line is. In other words, *slope* is defined as the ratio of vertical change (or rise) to horizontal change (or run) from one point on the line to another.

Slope is usually denoted by the letter m.

Furthermore, every line has a name. Its name is called an *equation*. Any two points on a given line will give the equation (the name). This means that the slope of a line is expressed as an equation:

$$m = \frac{\text{rise}}{\text{run}} = \frac{y_2 - y_1}{x_2 - x_1}$$

Let's look at an example. Let's assume that a line (l) passes through the two points (0, 0) and (2, 3).

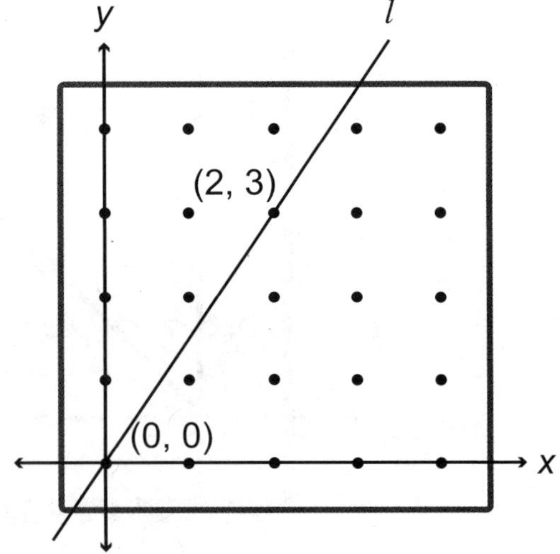

The slope would be $\frac{3}{2}$: $m = \frac{y_2 - y_1}{x_2 - x_1} = \frac{3-0}{2-0} = \frac{3}{2}$.

If we know the slope and one other point somewhere on the line—call it (x, y)—we can write an equation:

$$\frac{3}{2} = \frac{y-3}{x-2}$$

which simplifies to: $3x - 6 = 2y - 6$,

which equals $3x - 2y = 0$, the name of the line.

We can verify that this is the correct equation by substituting the two points we know are on the line for x and y. If each one gives us a true statement, then we know the equation is correct.

(2, 3) $3(2) - 2(3) = 0$

$6 - 6 = 0$

(0, 0) $3(0) - 2(0) = 0$

$0 - 0 = 0$

Name: ______________________ Date: ______________________

Given the Line, Find the Slope

Use a rubber band to make the line for each figure on your geoboard. Then find the slope.

1. **2.** **3.**

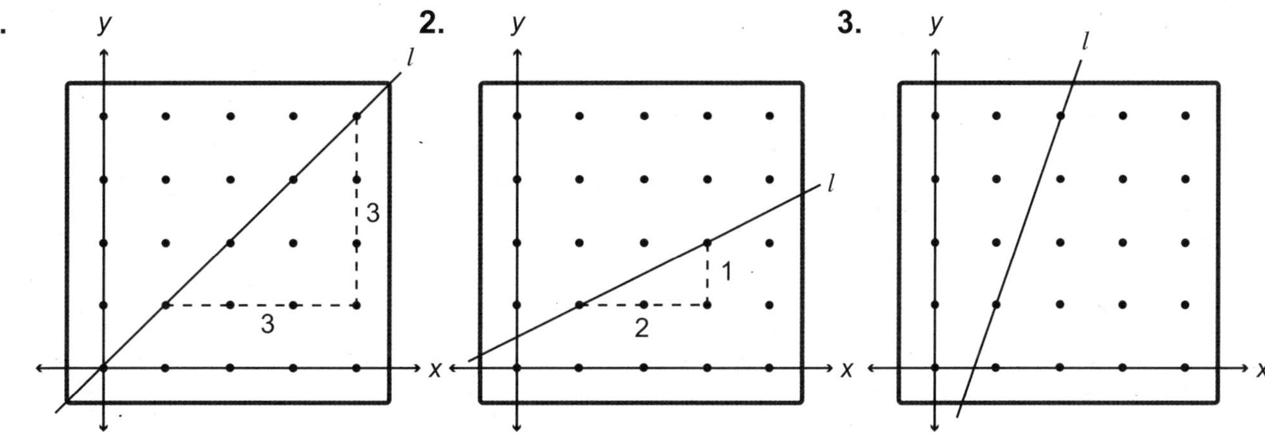

$m =$ ____________ $m =$ ____________ $m =$ ____________

4.

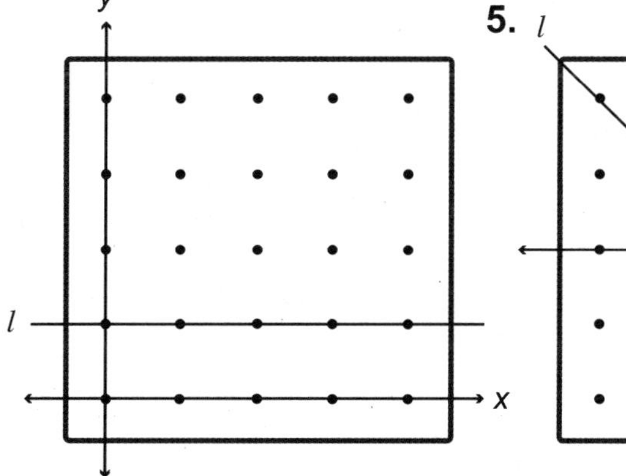

5.

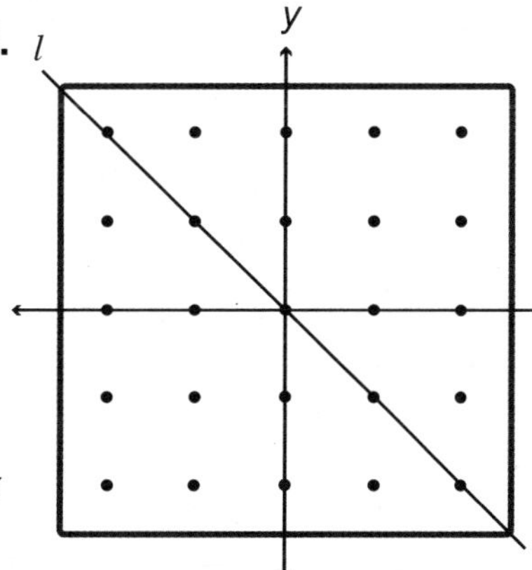

6.

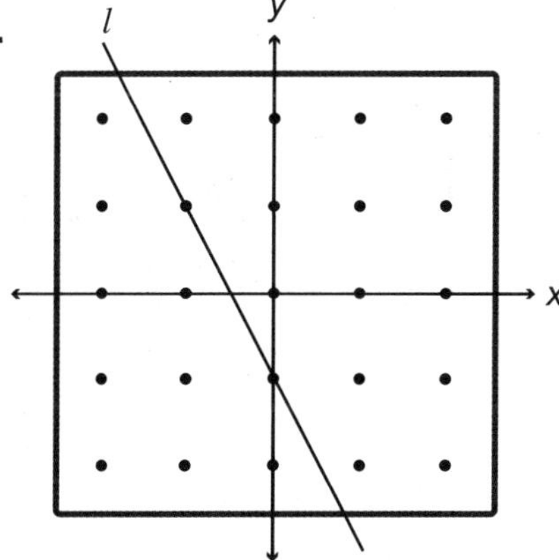

$m =$ ____________ $m =$ ____________ $m =$ ____________

PRACTICE

Name: ______________________ Date: ______________________

Given the Line, Write the Equation

Use a rubber band to make each line on your geoboard. Then write the equation of each line.

1.
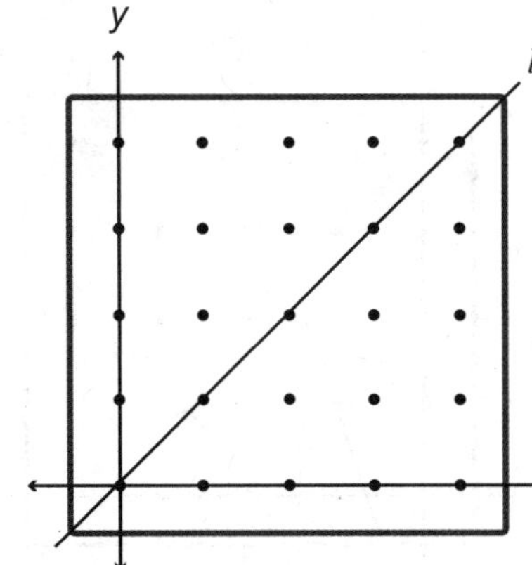

____

2.
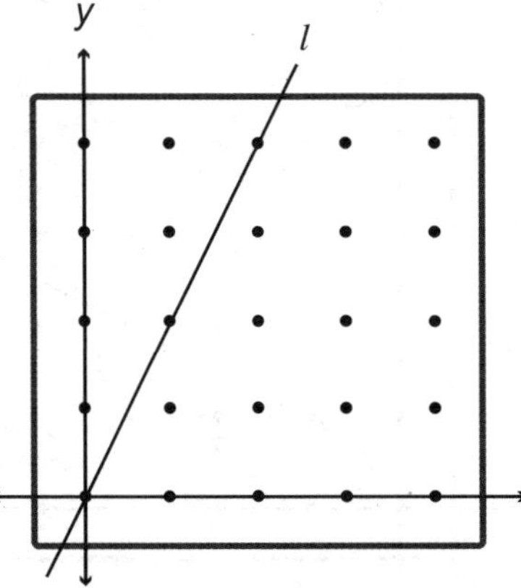

____

3.
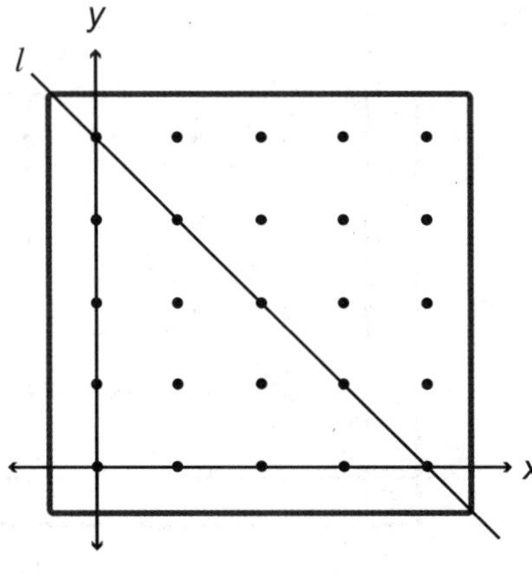

____

4.
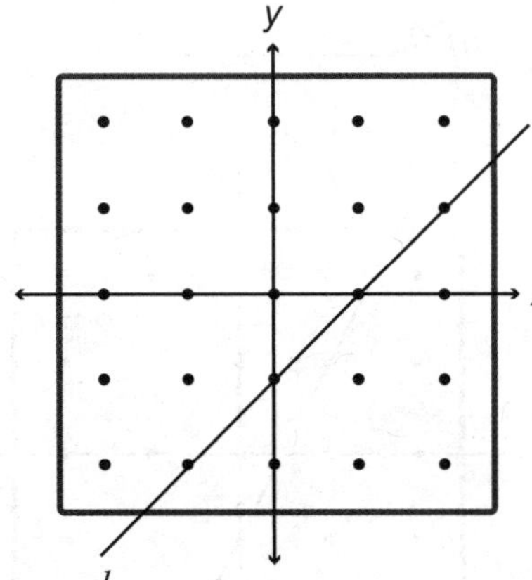

____

5.
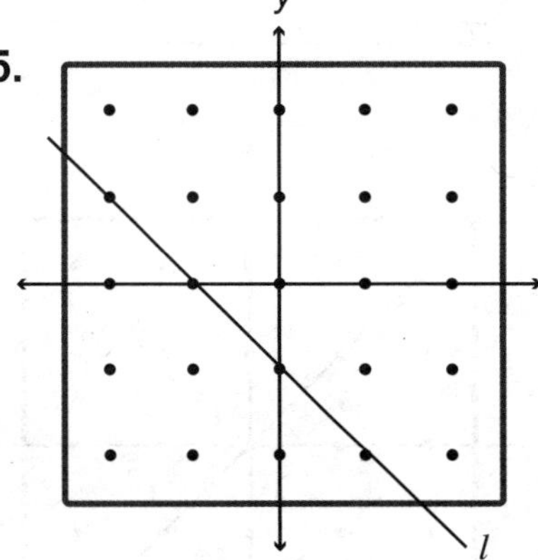

____

6.
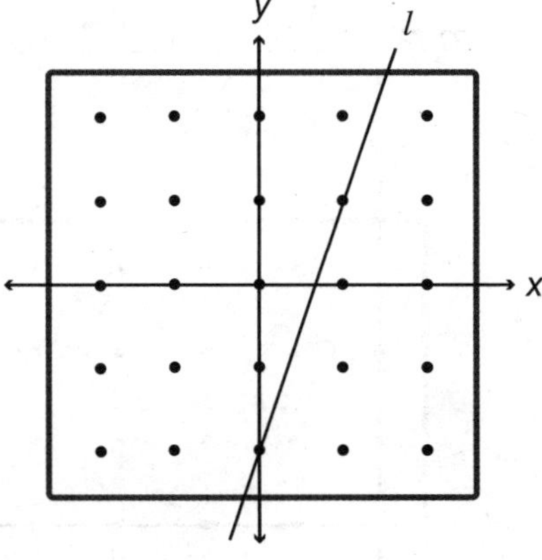

____

7.
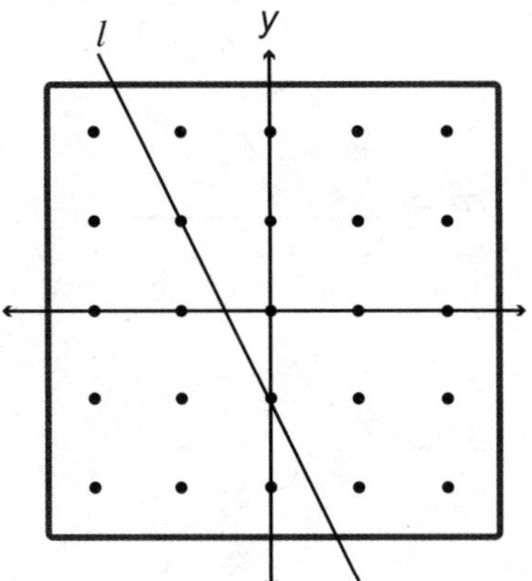

____

8.
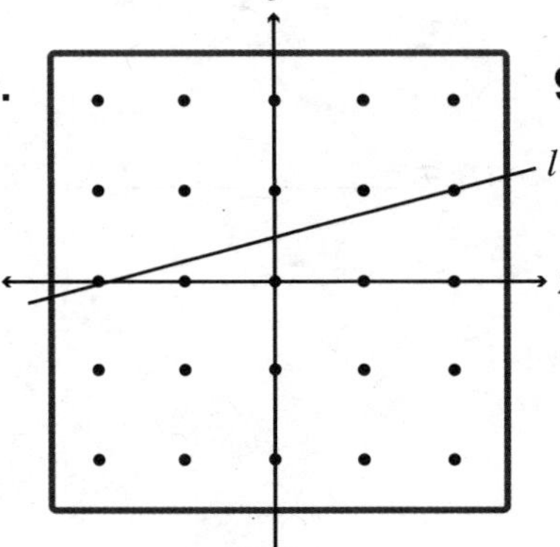

____

9.
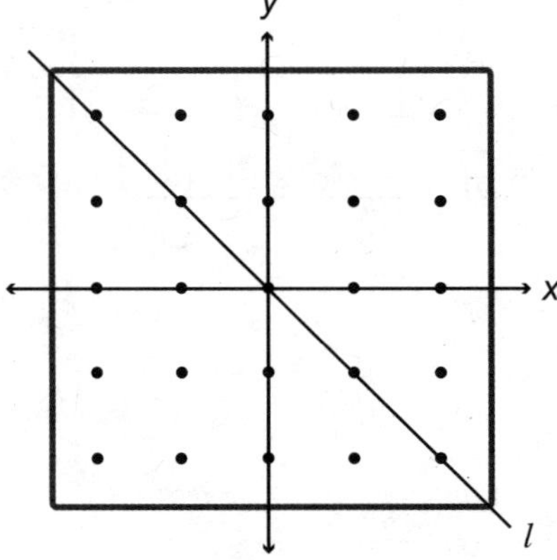

____

Name: ______________________ Date: ______________________

Given the Equation, Draw the Line

Draw the line for each equation given.

1. $x - y = 1$

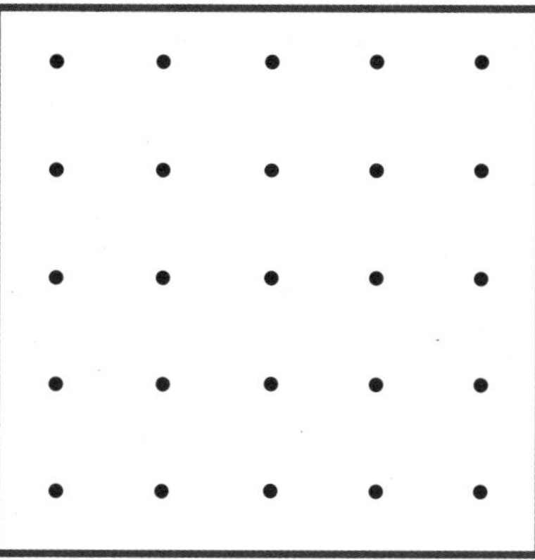

2. $2x - y = 4$

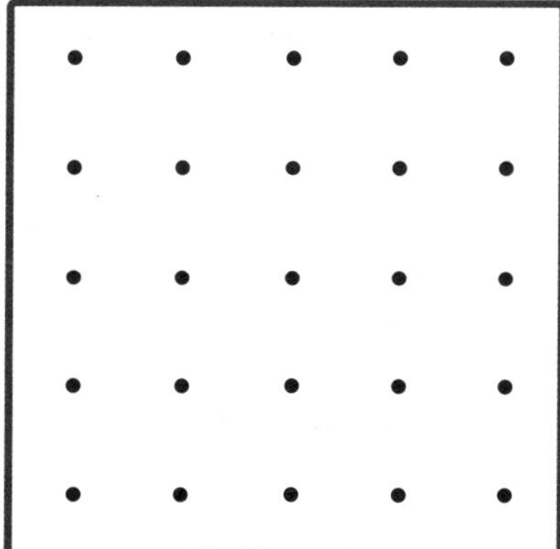

3. $3x = 4y - 1$

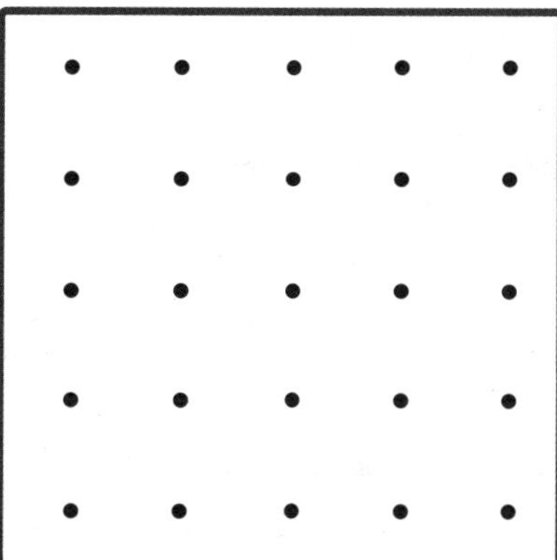

Name: ______________________ Date: ______________________

Slope

Find each slope (*m*). Write the equation of each line (*l*) below it.

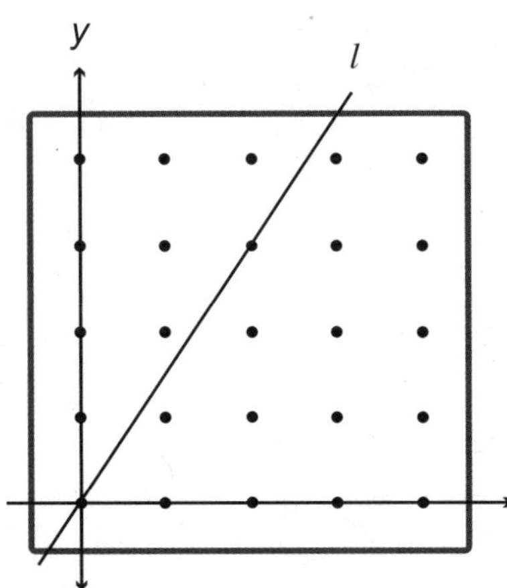

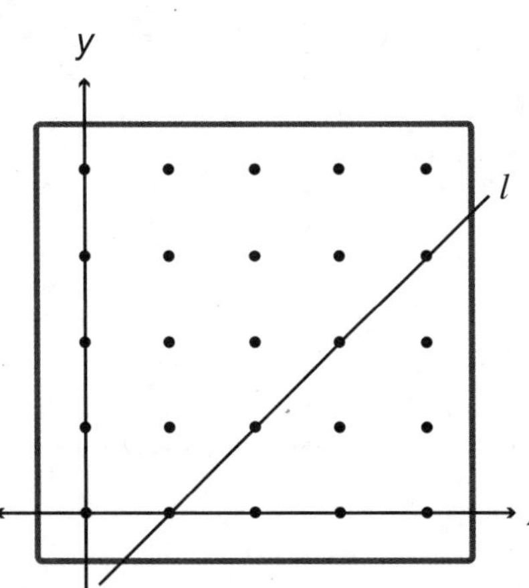

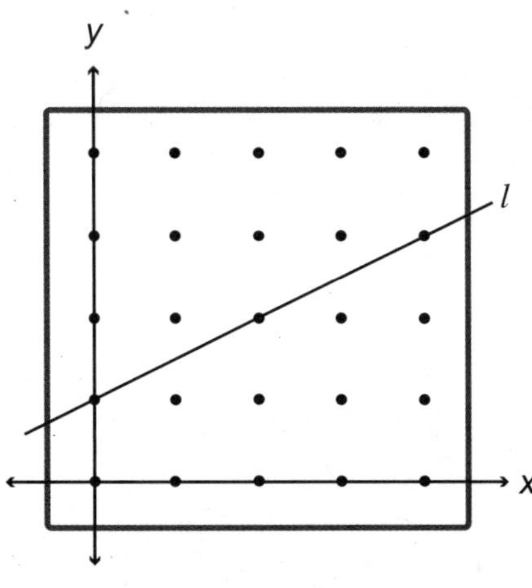

1. m = ______________

____

2. m = ______________

____

3. m = ______________

____

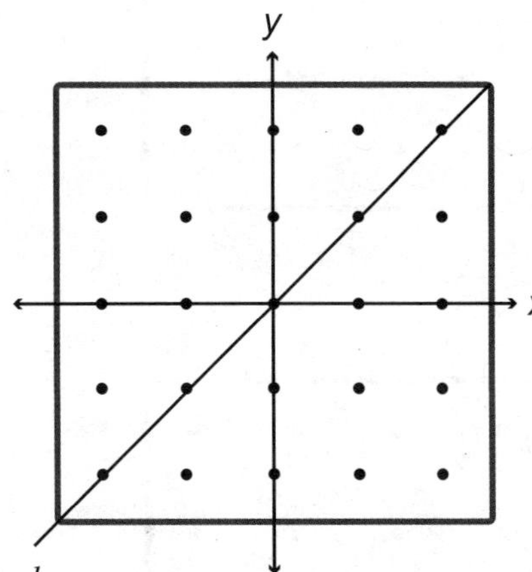

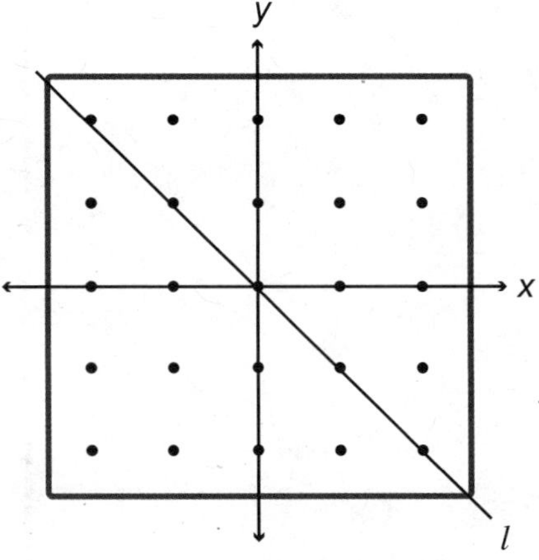

4. m = ______________

____

5. m = ______________

____

Chapter 7: Circle Geometry on the Geoboard

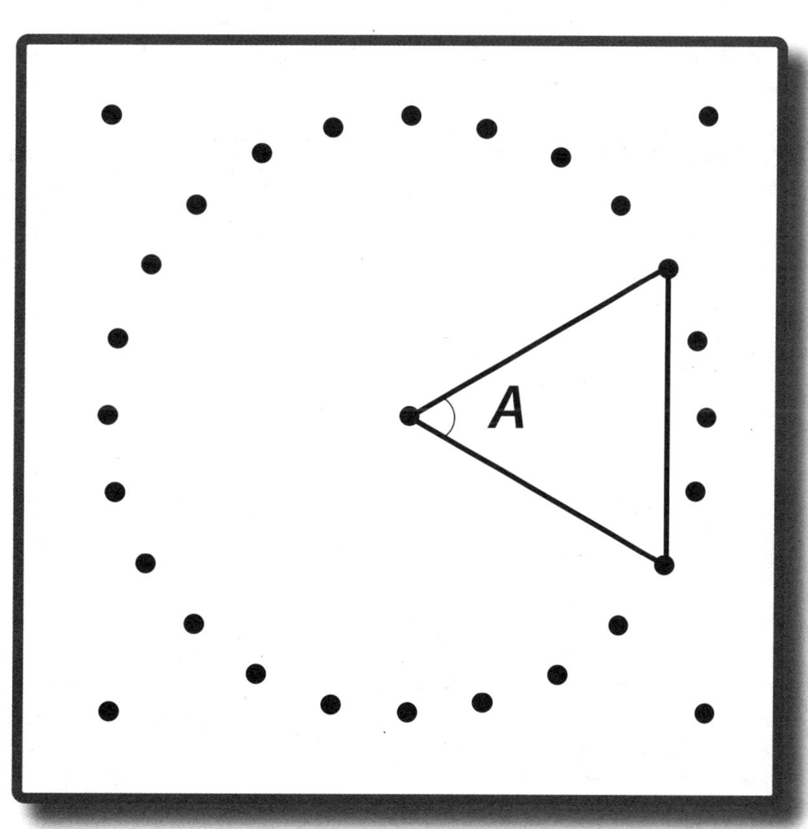

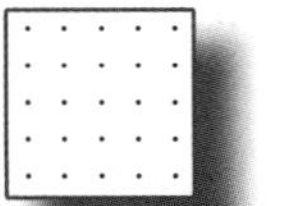

7.1 Angles and Arcs

Main Ideas

Most 25-pin geoboards are two-sided—rectangular on one side and circular on the opposite side. Notice that there are 24 pins on the circle. Since there are 360 degrees in a circle, the number of degrees between each pin is 15 degrees. Notice also that there is one pin at the center of the circle.

Angles formed with the center of a circle are called *central angles*. Angles formed with a vertex on a circle are called *inscribed angles*.

An *arc* is a portion of the circumference of a circle. The part of the circle that is intercepted by two lines that form an angle is called an *intercepted arc*. The measure of an arc in degrees is the measure of the corresponding central angle.

A *radius* (plural: *radii*) is a line segment from the center of a circle to any point on the circle.

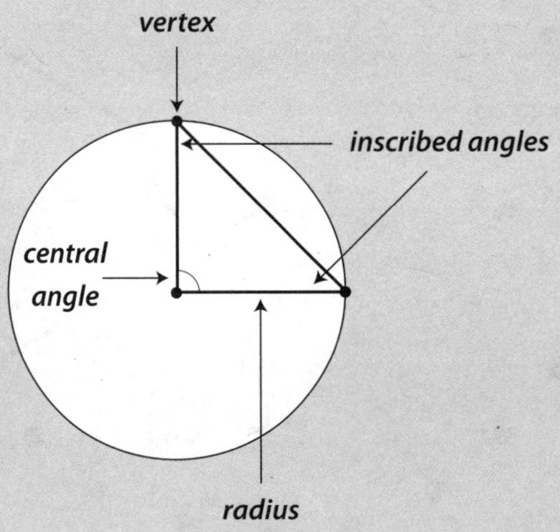

Name: ______________________ Date: ______________________

Measure the Central Angle

Using your circular geoboard, make each triangle shown below and calculate the central angle. Remember that the space between each pin on the circle measures 15 degrees. (Use a protractor if necessary.)

1.

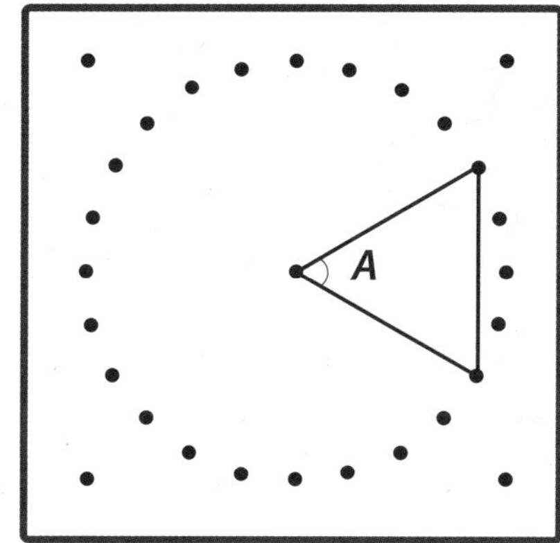

Angle *A* = __________ degrees

2.

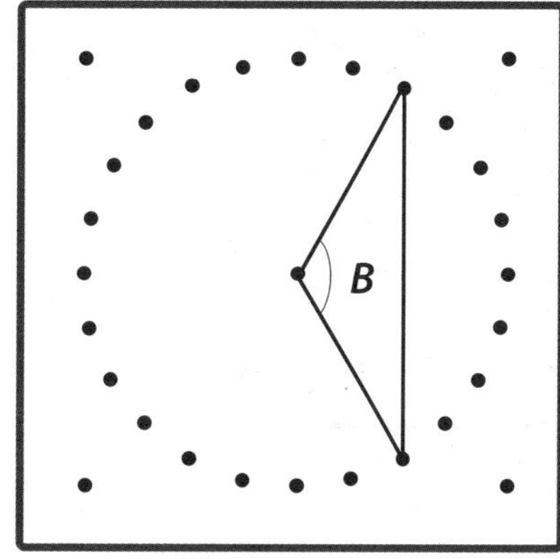

Angle *B* = __________ degrees

3.

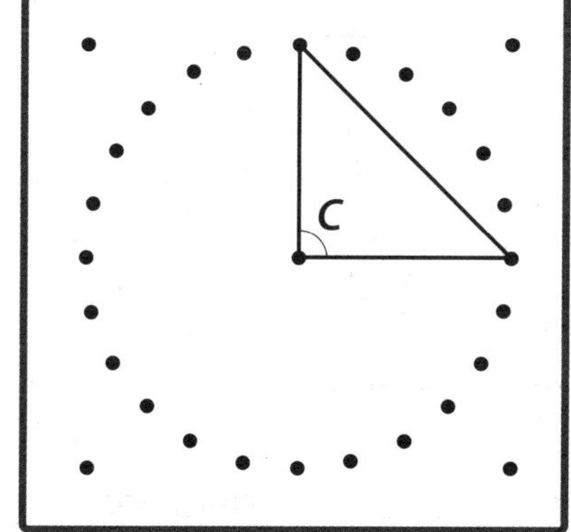

Angle *C* = __________ degrees

4.

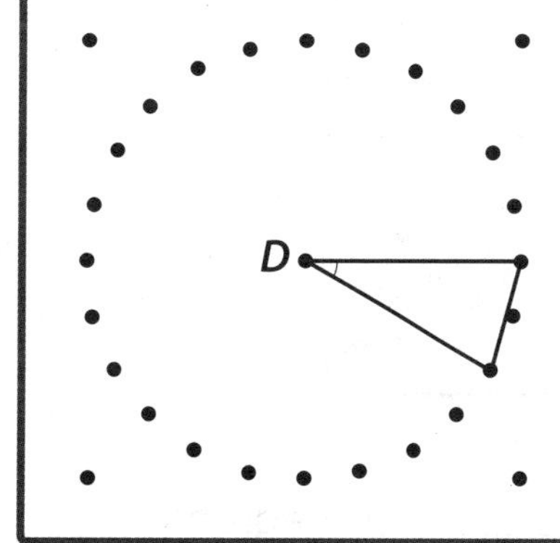

Angle *D* = __________ degrees

5. Can you find a relationship between the central angle and the portion of the circumference (the arc) intercepted by that angle?

____

____

Name: ______________________ Date: ______________________

What Is the Measure of the Inscribed Angle?

Find the measure of the inscribed angle *a* in each of the figures below.

1.

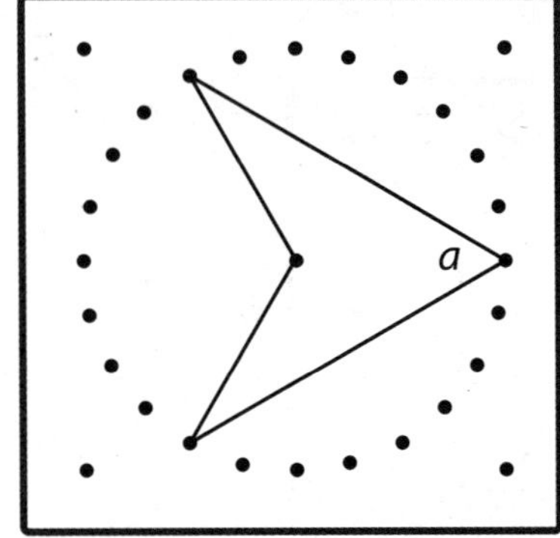

Angle *a* = __________ degrees

2.

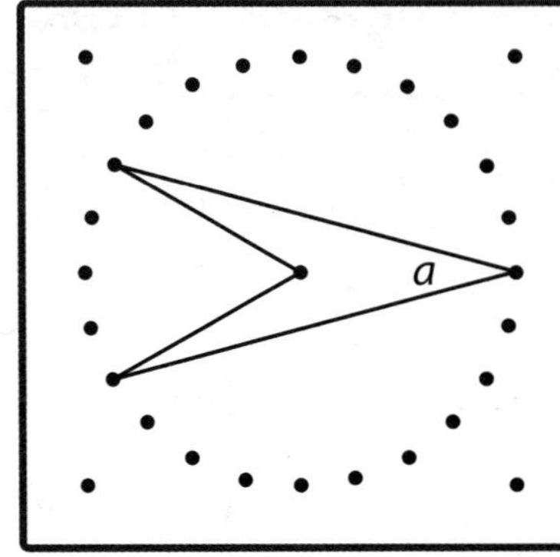

Angle *a* = __________ degrees

3.

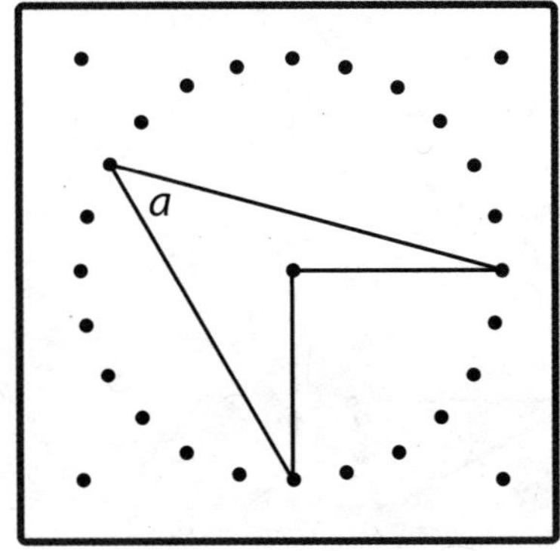

Angle *a* = __________ degrees

4.

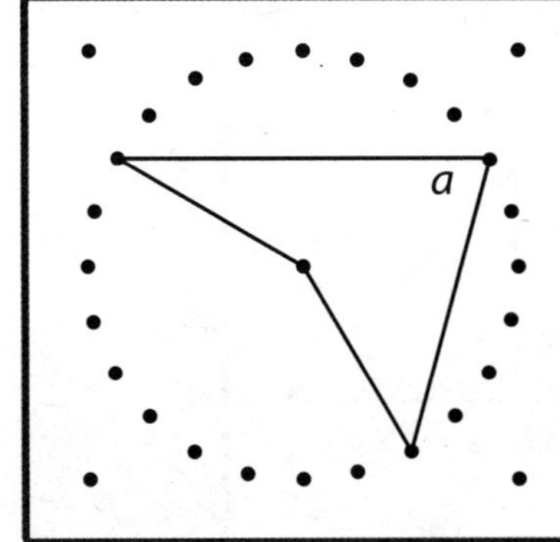

Angle *a* = __________ degrees

5. For each figure, how does the inscribed angle compare to the measure of the central angle? ______________________________

____

Name: ______________________ Date: ______________________

What Is the Sum of the Measures of the Angles?

Study the triangles inscribed in the circles below and see whether you can figure out the answer to this question: WHAT IS THE SUM OF THE MEASURES OF THE ANGLES OF A TRIANGLE?

1.

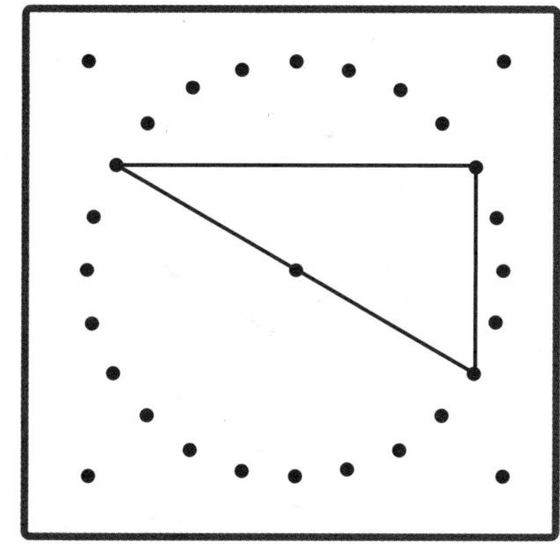

Angle sum = __________ degrees

2.

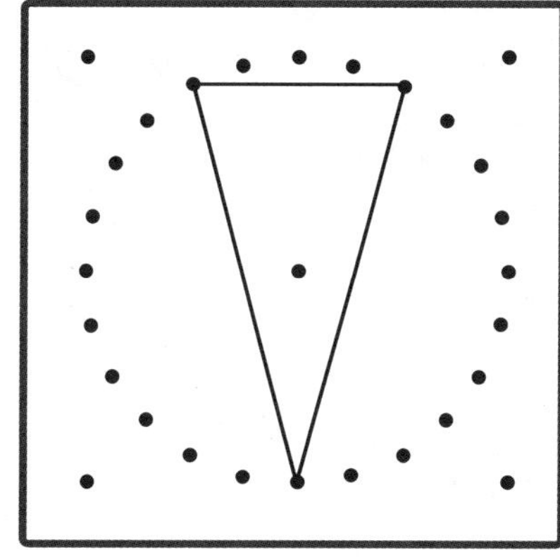

Angle sum = __________ degrees

3.

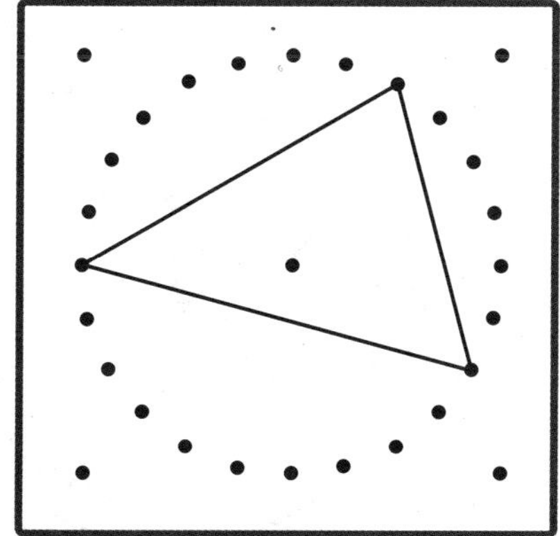

Angle sum = __________ degrees

4.

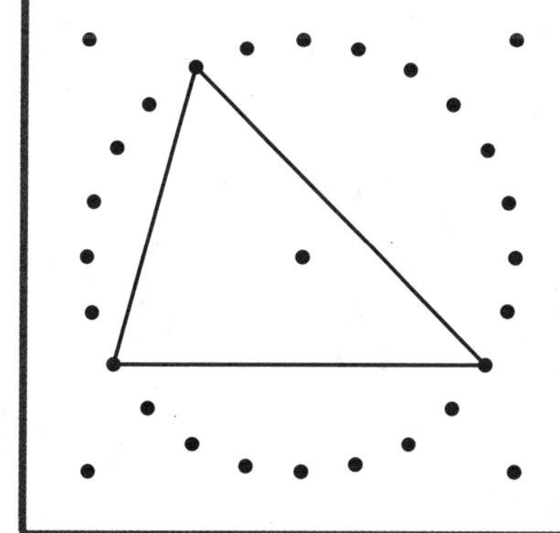

Angle sum = __________ degrees

5. The sum of the measures of the angles of a triangle is ______________________.

PRACTICE

Name: ______________________ Date: ______________________

The Angles of the Hands of a Clock

Find the angles formed by the hands on a clock as indicated. Use the pictures below to help you solve these problems.

1.

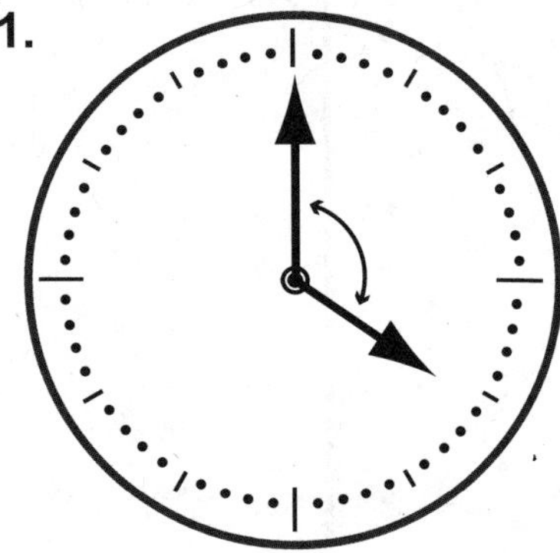

Angle = __________

2.

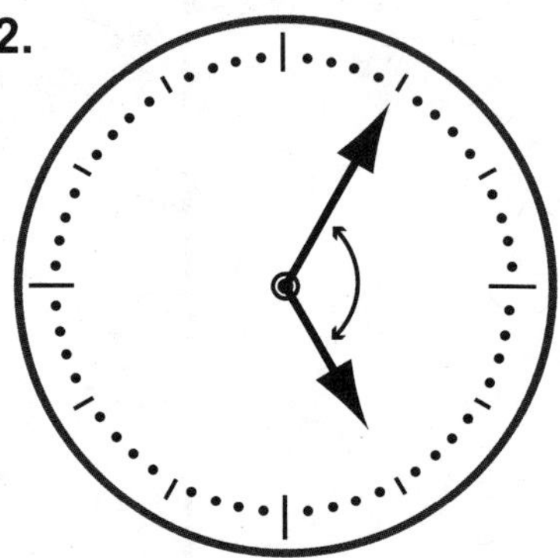

Angle = __________

3.

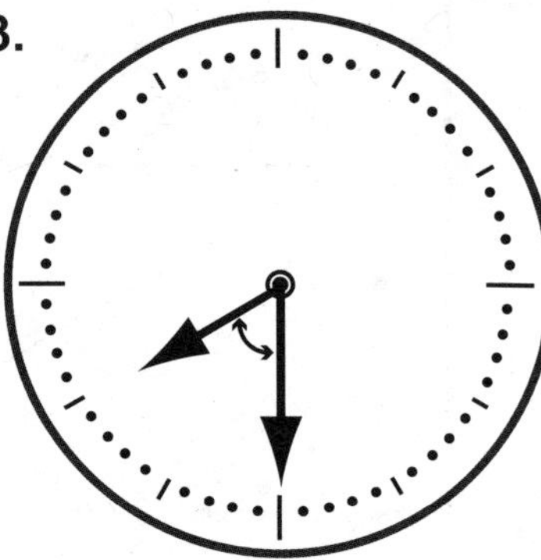

Angle = __________

4.

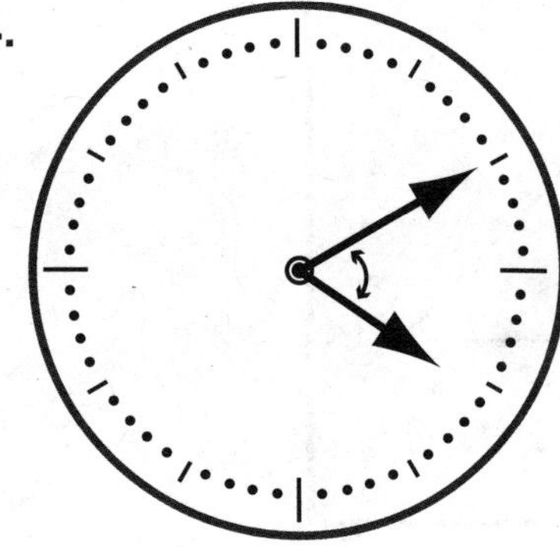

Angle = __________

5.

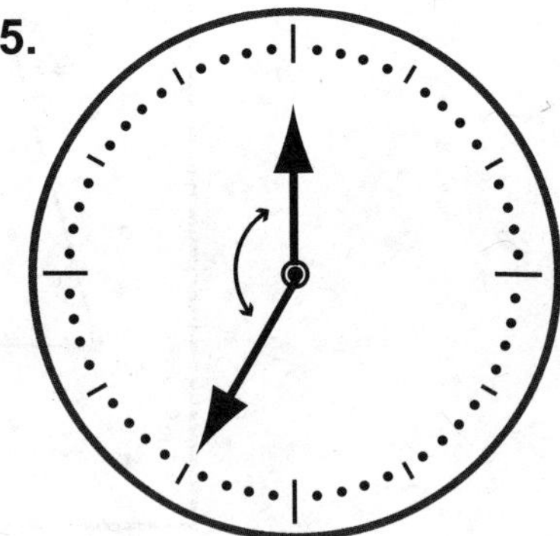

Angle = __________

6.

Angle = __________

Name: ______________________ Date: ______________________

What Are the Measures of the Interior Angles?

Find the interior angles of the figures below. Use what you have learned from the previous problems involving circles and angle measures.

1.

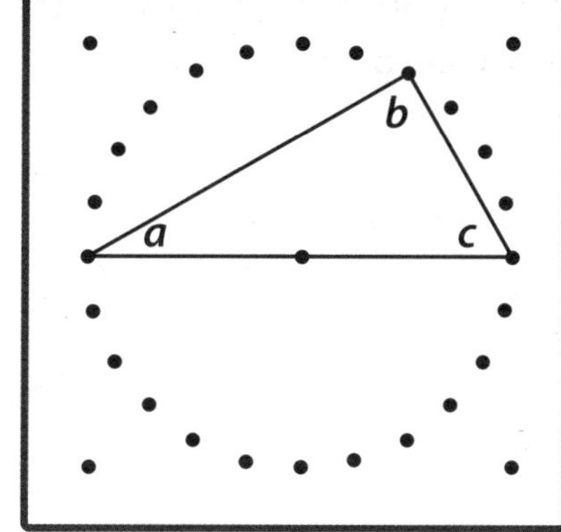

Angle *a* = __________ degrees

Angle *b* = __________ degrees

Angle *c* = __________ degrees

2.

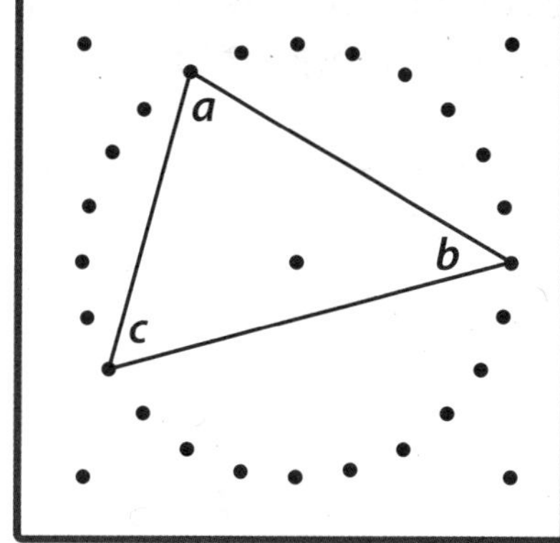

Angle *a* = __________ degrees

Angle *b* = __________ degrees

Angle *c* = __________ degrees

3.

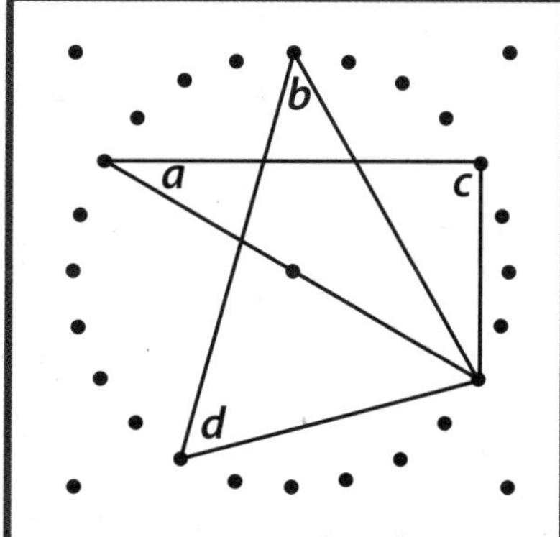

Angle *a* = __________ degrees

Angle *b* = __________ degrees

Angle *c* = __________ degrees

Angle *d* = __________ degrees

4.

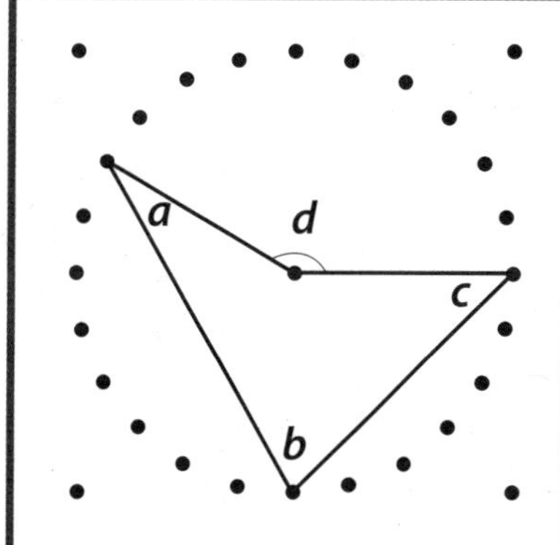

Angle *a* = __________ degrees

Angle *b* = __________ degrees

Angle *c* = __________ degrees

Angle *d* = __________ degrees

Name: ______________________ Date: ______________

What Kind of Triangle Is It?

Recall that triangles are classified by their side lengths (scalene, isosceles, equilateral) and by the types of angles that form them (acute, obtuse, and right).

Now study, or build on your geoboard, each inscribed triangle shown below. Then identify what type of triangle it is. The first one has been done for you.

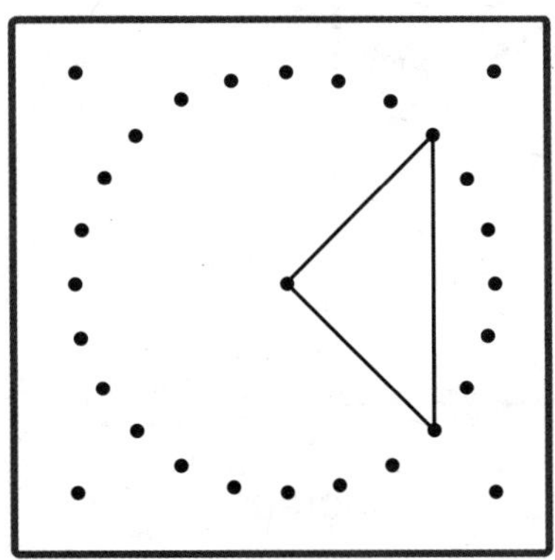

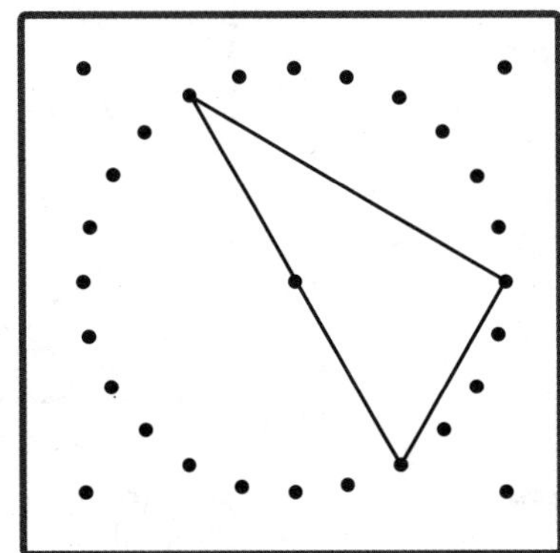

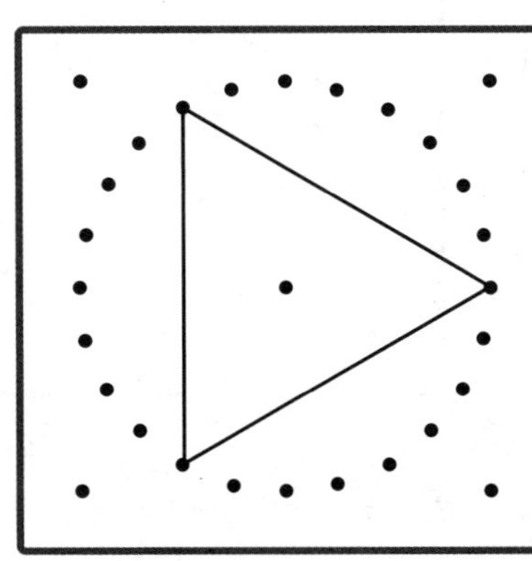

1. isosceles, right

2. ______________

3. ______________

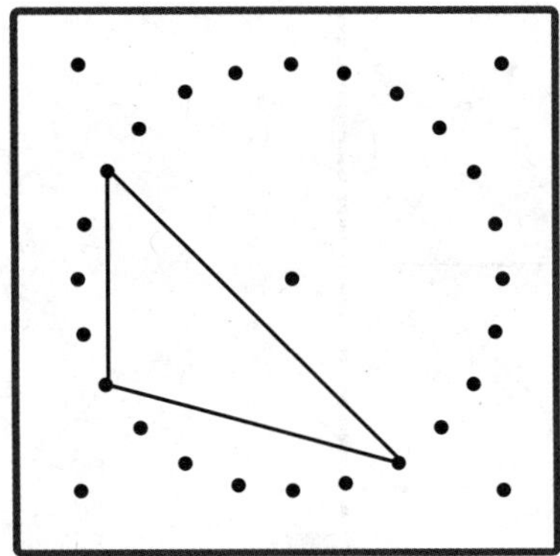

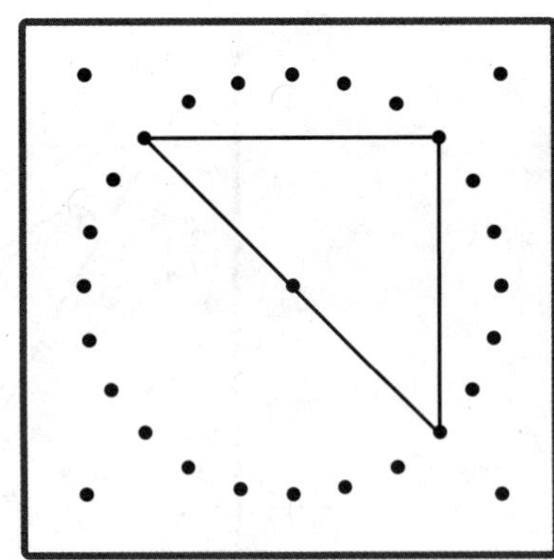

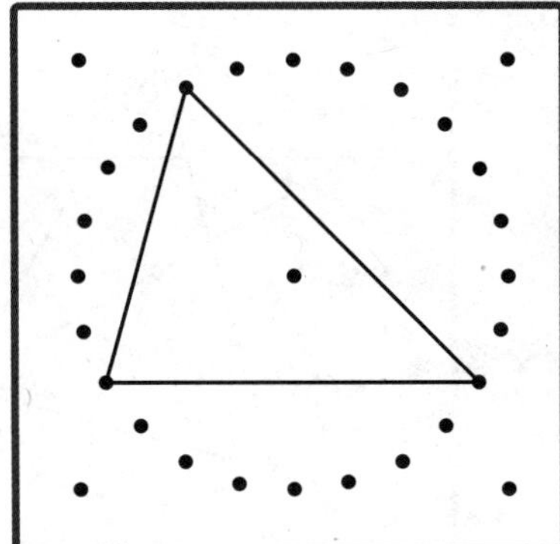

4. ______________

5. ______________

6. ______________

Name: ______________________ Date: ______________________

Intercepted Arcs

Recall that:

- An *arc* is a portion of the circumference of a circle.
- An *intercepted arc* is the part of the circle that is inside the angle formed by two lines that cross the circle.
- The measure of an *arc* in degrees is the measure of the corresponding central angle.

Study the two figures below and answer the questions that follow.

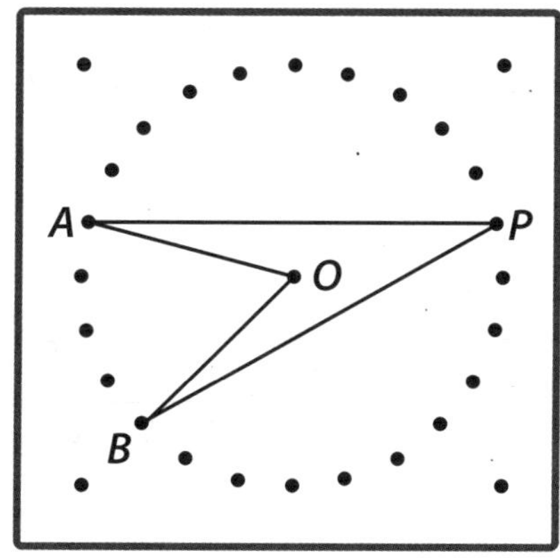

Figure 1

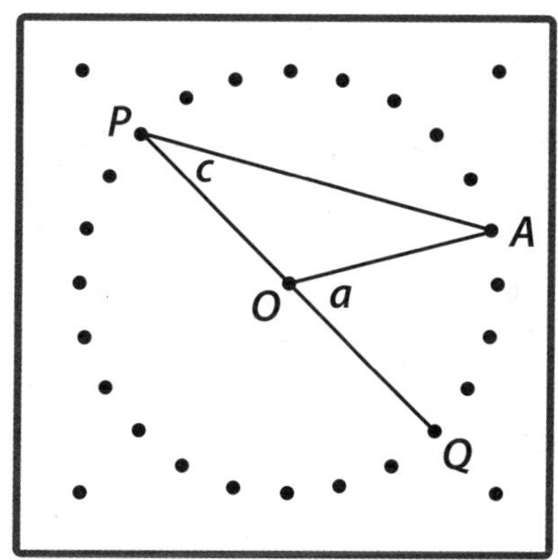

Figure 2

1. In Figure 1:

a. Measure of angle *APB* = ____________ measure of angle *AOB*

b. Measure of angle *AOB* = ____________ degrees

c. Measure of arc *AB* = ____________ degrees

2. In Figure 2, what is the arc intercepted by angle AOQ? ________________

3. In Figure 2, if the measure of angle *a* = 60 degrees, what is the measure of angle *c*?

____________ degrees

Name: ____________________ Date: ____________________

Circle Geometry

Circle the correct answers.

1. All radii of a given circle have equal lengths. **True** **False**

2. The central angle of a circle is an angle whose vertex is the center of the circle. **True** **False**

3. The lengths of the radii of all circles are equal. **True** **False**

4. The measure of any inscribed angle is always equal to $\frac{1}{2}$ of the measure of the central angle. **True** **False**

5. The diameter of a circle always inscribes an arc of 180 degrees. **True** **False**

6. Any triangle drawn inside a circle is a right triangle. **True** **False**

7. No central angle can measure more than 120 degrees. **True** **False**

8. If two lines pass through the same circle, their point of intersection will be the center of the circle. **True** **False**

9. At one o'clock, the hands of the clock determine an angle whose central angle equals 15 degrees. **True** **False**

10. The sum of any two central angles is always equal to 360 degrees. **True** **False**

Answers

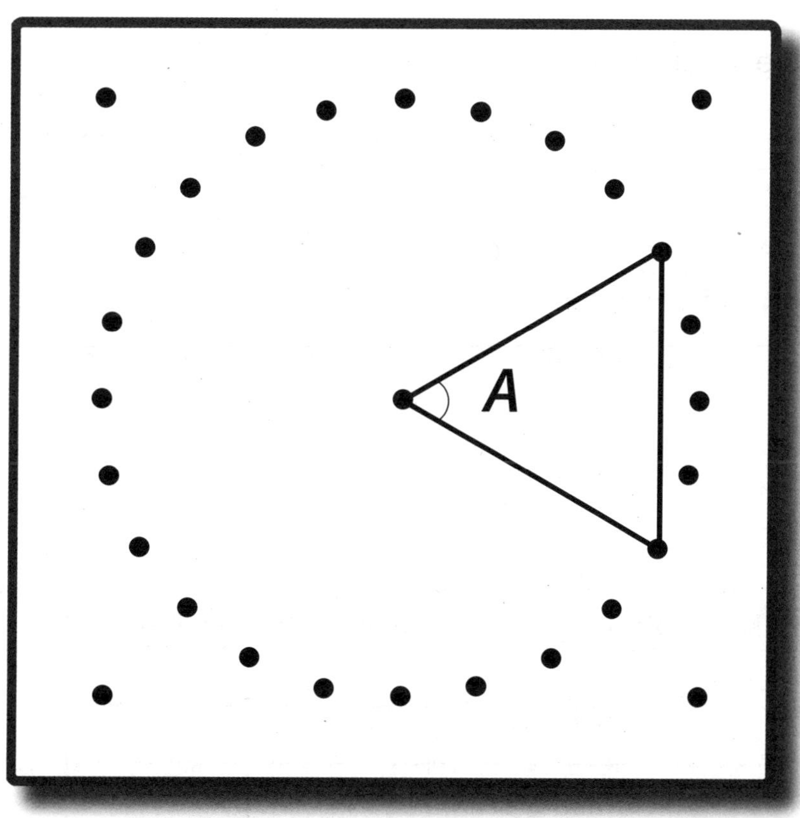

Answers

Chapter 1: Finding Area on the Geoboard

Page 5:

All answers are in square units.

1. 5 **2.** 6 **3.** 6 **4.** 8 **5.** 8 **6.** 12 **7.** $4\frac{1}{2}$ **8.** 10 **9.** 8

Page 6:

All answers are in square units.

1. $4\frac{1}{2}$ **2.** $3\frac{1}{2}$ **3.** 5 **4.** 4 **5.** 8 **6.** 2 **7.** 4 **8.** 7

Page 7:

All answers are in square units.

1. 4 **2.** 4 **3.** 3 **4.** 8 **5.** 7 **6.** 6 **7.** 9 **8.** 2 **9.** 5

Page 8: Teacher check.

Page 12:

Shape	# Pegs Inside	Scalene	Isosceles	Equilateral
A	1	X		
B	3	X		
C	0	X		
D	1		X	
E	1		X	
F	0		X	
G	3		X	
H	3	X		
I	0	X		

Page 14:

Shape	# Pegs Inside	Acute	Obtuse	Right	Isosceles	Scalene	Equilateral
A	3	X				X	
B	0			X	X		
C	1		X			X	
D	1	X				X	
E	1		X			X	
F	1	X			X		
G	3			X	X		
H	0		X		X		
I	1	X			X		

Page 15:

1. No **2.** No **3.** Yes **4.** No **5.** No **6.** No **7.** No

8. False **9.** False **10.** False

Page 17:

No, it is not a rhombus. It does not have four congruent sides. Adjacent sides are not equal in length.

Page 18:

Answers may vary. Possible answers include:

1. (A) It is a parallelogram, (B) has 4 right angles, and (C) adjacent sides are equal.
2. (A) It is a parallelogram, (B) has 4 right angles, and (C) adjacent sides do not have to be equal.
3. (A) It is a quadrilateral, (B) with only one pair of parallel sides, and (C) always has an obtuse angle.
4. (A) It is a parallelogram, (B) with all four sides equal in length, and (C) has two obtuse angles.
5. No
6. Yes, but not on the geoboard.
7. Yes

Answers (cont.)

Page 20:

Figures A and D are concave; B and C are convex. Concave shapes are "caved in."

Page 21:

1. True	**2.** False	**3.** False	**4.** True	**5.** True
6. False	**7.** False	**8.** True	**9.** True	**10.** False
11. True	**12.** True	**13.** True	**14.** No	**15.** Yes

Page 25:

1. Set A: Area:1, 4, 16; Formula: Area = side squared
2. Set B: Area: 4, 8, 3; Formula: Area = base × height
3. Set C: Area: 2, 4, 2; Formula: Area = $\frac{1}{2}$(base × height)

Page 26:

1. 4 **2.** 3 **3.** 9 **1–3.** Area = base × height

4. 6 **5.** 5 **6.** 7 **4–6.** Area = $\frac{1}{2}$(base 1 + base 2) × height

Page 28:

1. Set A: The rubber band touches the same number of pins in each shape. (They are all triangles.) They each have a different number of pins inside and a different area.
2. Set B: They are all squares. They each have a different number of pins inside and a different area.
3. Set C: They are all pentagons. They each have a different number of pins inside and a different area.
4. Conclusions will vary, but one conclusion is that the area of a shape is affected by two things: the number of pegs touched by the rubber band and the number of pegs inside the shape. (The area formula is yet to be discovered in a lesson that follows.)

Page 29–30:

1. Teacher check.
2. Teacher check.
3. Teacher check.
4. Teacher check.
5. $A = \frac{1}{2}N + (I - 1)$, if A = area, P = the number of pins touched by the rubber band, and I = the number of pins inside the shape.

Page 32:

1. The area of the square on the hypotenuse equals the sum of the areas of the other two squares: $\sqrt{2}$. The sum of the squares of the lengths of the two sides equals the square of the length of the hypotenuse.

2. 13 units **3.** 24 units **4.** 5 units

Page 34:

1. 8 units **2.** 16 units **3.** 10 units **4.** 14 units **5.** 16 units

6. 14 units **7.** $3 + \sqrt{5}$ **8.** $5 + \sqrt{17}$ **9.** $4 + \sqrt{8}$

Page 35:

1. 44 ft **2.** 178 cm

Page 36: Teacher check.

Page 37:

1. 6 **2.** Yes **3.** Yes: 1, 2, 4, 5, 8, 9; No: 3, 6, 7

4. Yes. Possible answers:

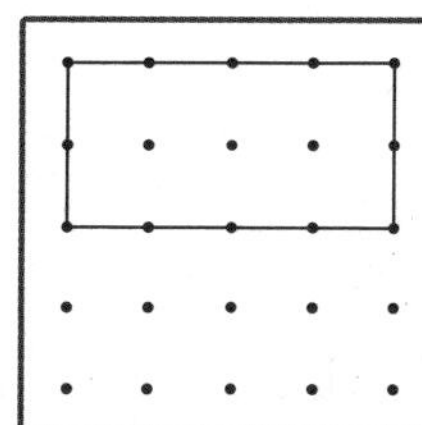
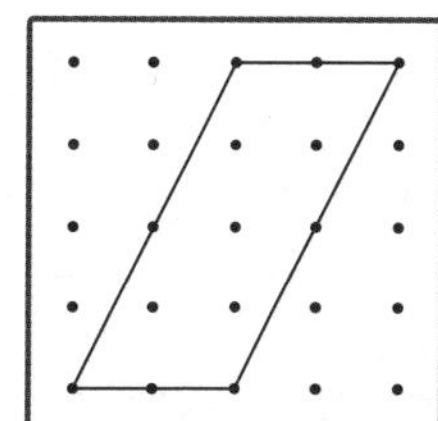
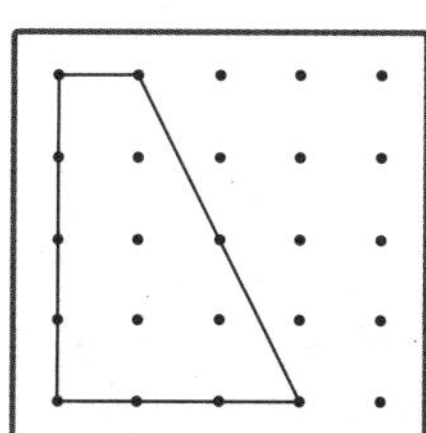

5. Yes, a 4 × 4 square has an area of 16 and a perimeter of 16.

6. Yes. Teacher check.
7. The areas of the two triangles are the same. Their perimeters are also the same.
8. The area of the larger triangle is four times the area of the smaller triangle.

Page 39:

L (length of side)	1	2	3	4	5	6	7	8
N (number of squares)	1	4	9	16	25	36	49	64

The formula is $N = L^2$.

Page 40:

Shape	*S* (number of sides)	*N* (number of diagonals)
Triangle	3	0
Square	4	2
Pentagon	5	5
Hexagon	6	9
Other (your choice):		
Heptagon	7	14
Octagon	8	20

The formula is $N = \frac{S(S-3)}{2}$.

Page 41:

B (length of base)	1	2	3	4	5	6	7	8
T (number of triangles)	1	4	9	16	25	36	49	64

The formula is $T = B^2$.

Page 48:

1. 10

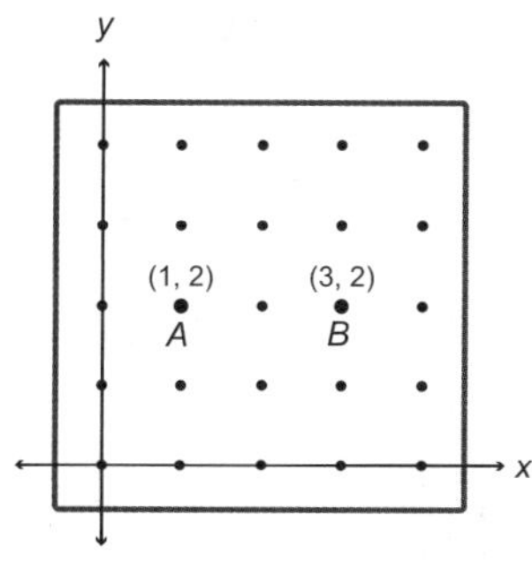

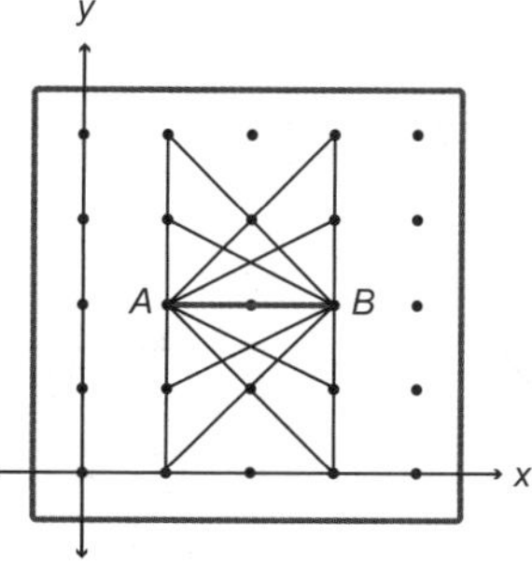

2. 5

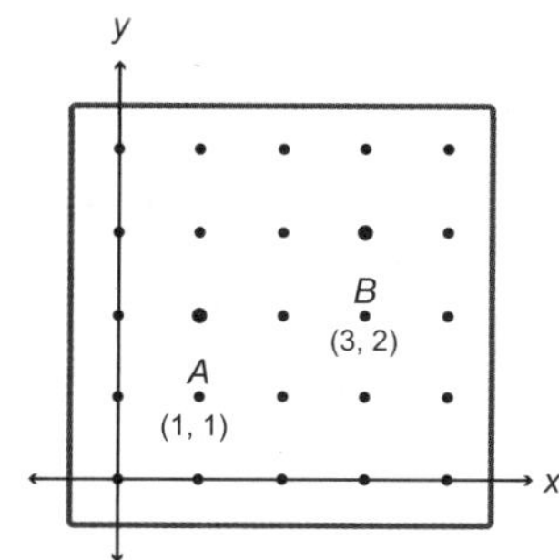

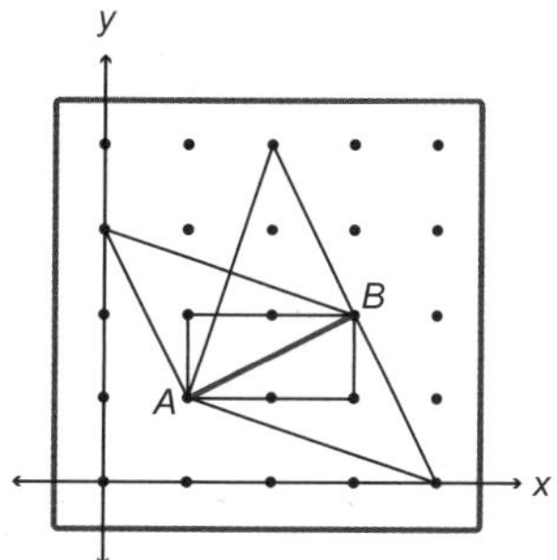

Page 52:

1.

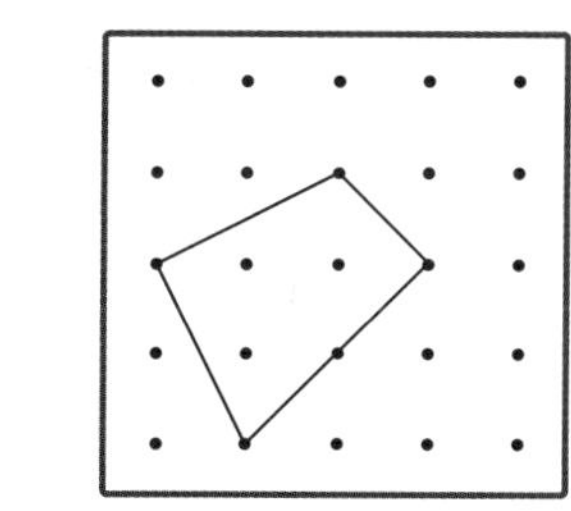

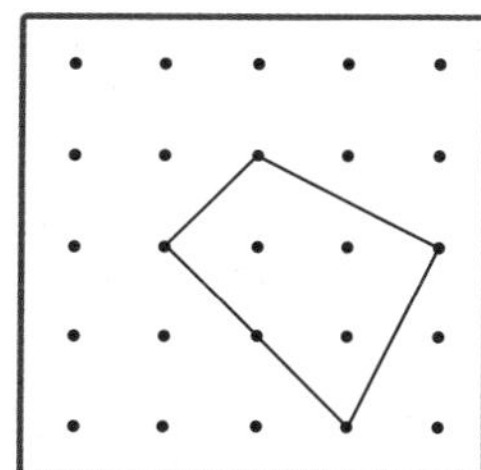

2.

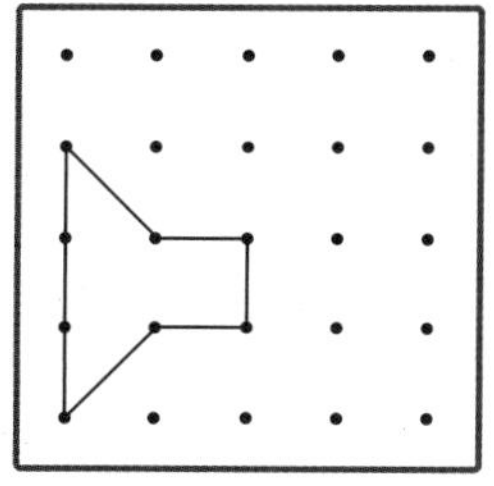

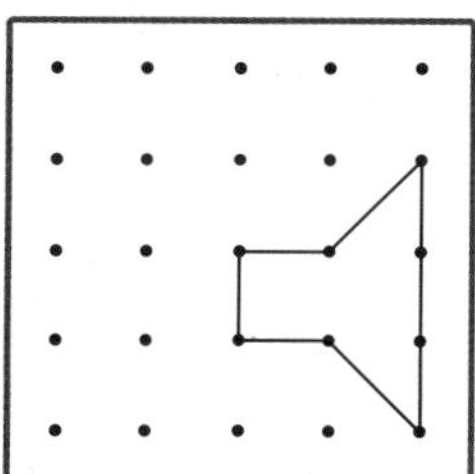

3.

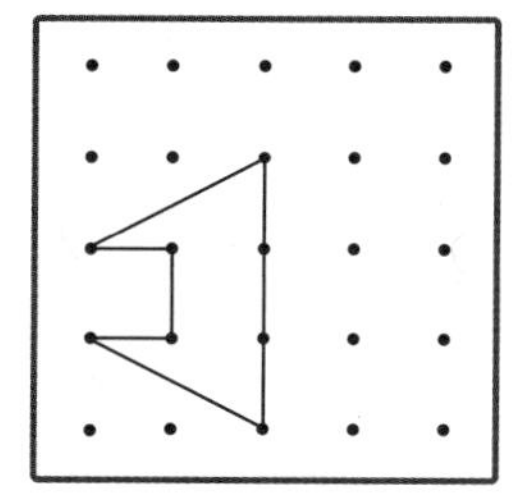

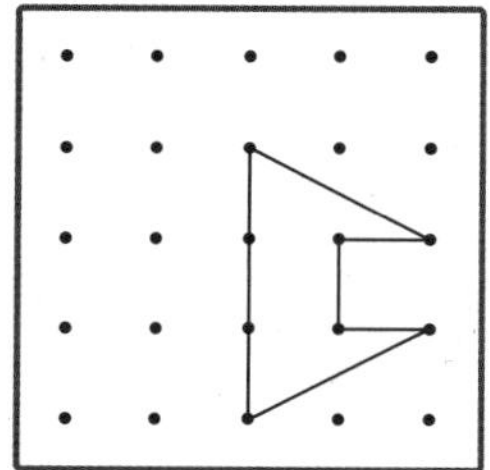

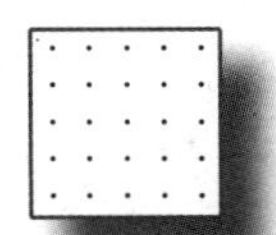

Answers (cont.)

Page 53:

1.

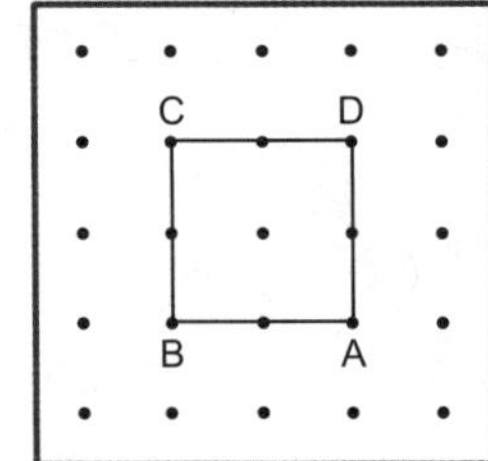

2.

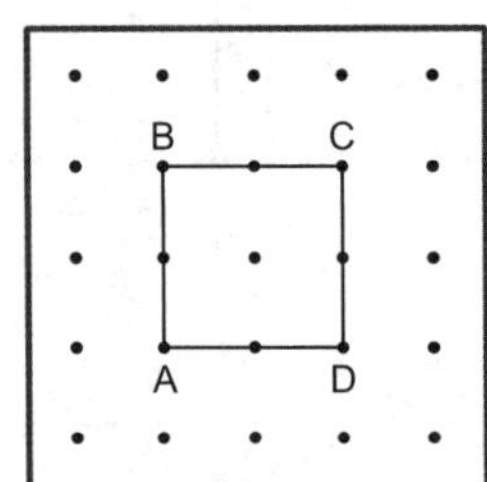

Page 54:

Column B | **Column C**

1.

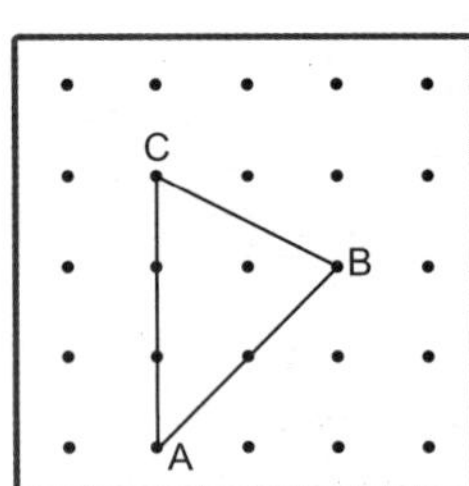

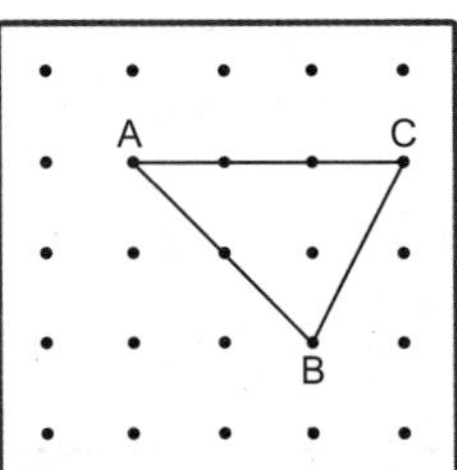

2.

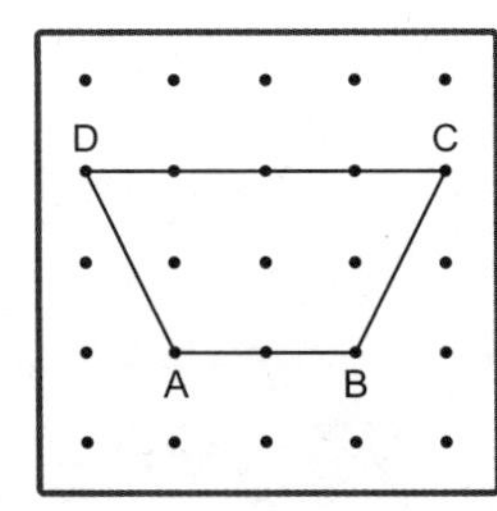

D
A
B
C

3.

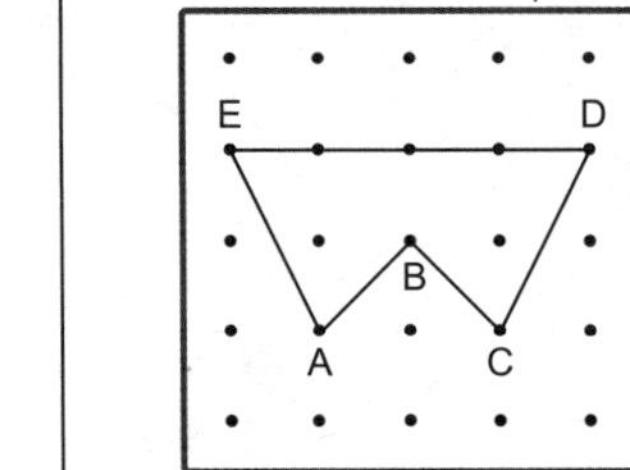

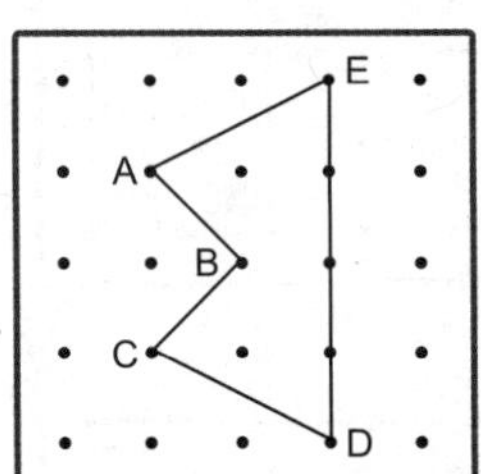

Page 55:

1.

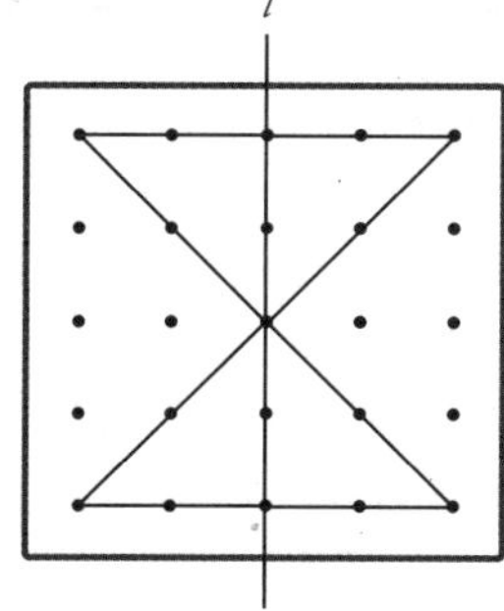

2.

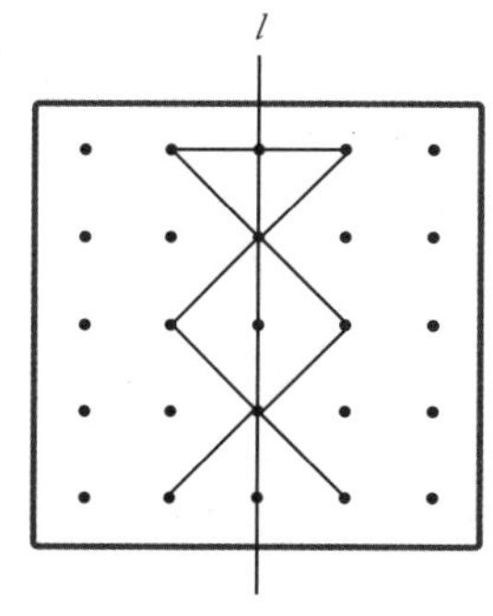

3.

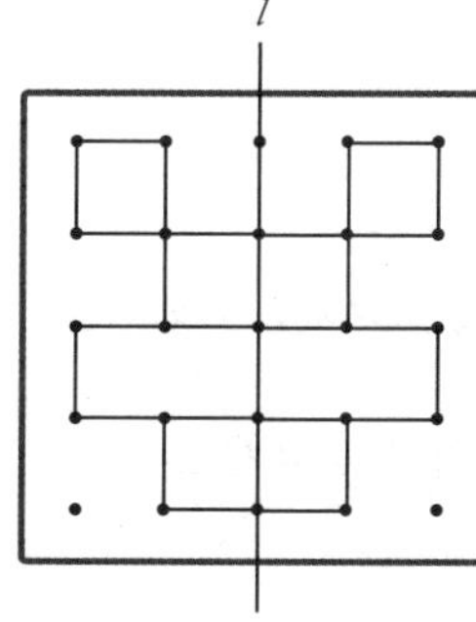

4.

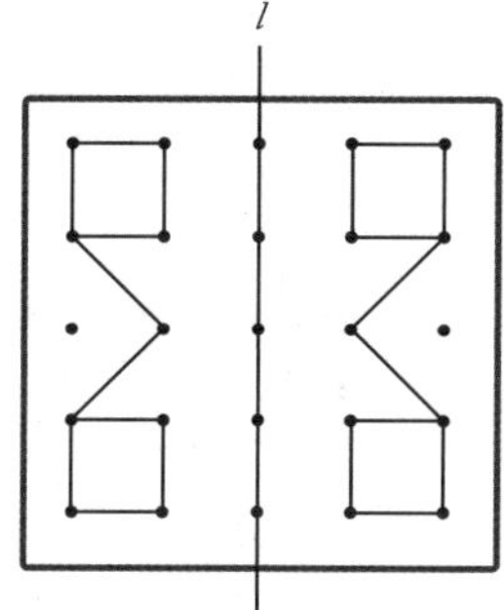

5.

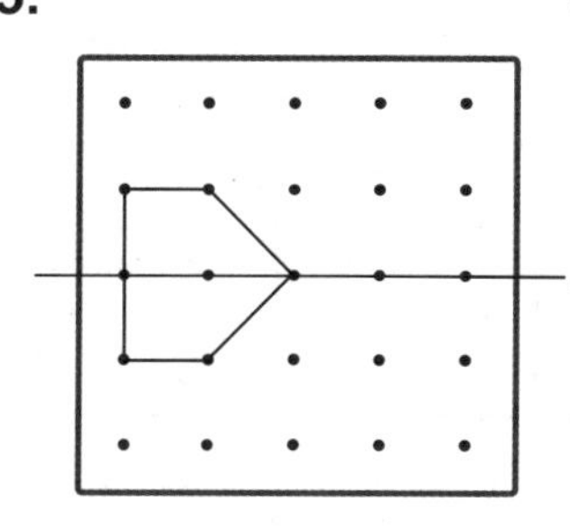

6.

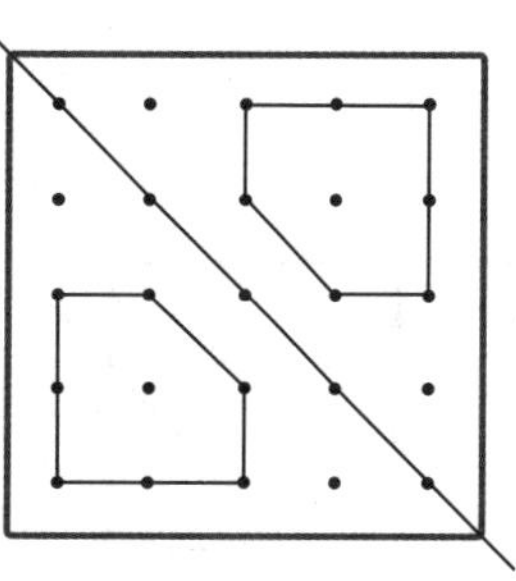

Page 56:

1. True **2.** False **3.** No

Page 59:

1. 1 **2.** $\frac{1}{2}$ **3.** 3 **4.** 0 **5.** ${}^{-}1$ **6.** ${}^{-}2$

Page 60:

1. $y = x$, or $x - y = 0$

2. $y = 2x$, or $2x - y = 0$

3. $y = {}^{-}x + 4$, or $x + y = 4$

4. $y = x - 1$, or $x - y = 1$

5. $y = {}^{-}x - 1$, or $x + y = {}^{-}1$

6. $y = 3x - 2$, or $3x - y = 2$

7. $y = {}^{-}2x - 1$, or $2x + y = {}^{-}1$

8. $x - 4y = {}^-2$, or $4y = x + 2$

9. $y = {}^-x$, or $x + y = 0$

Page 61:

1.

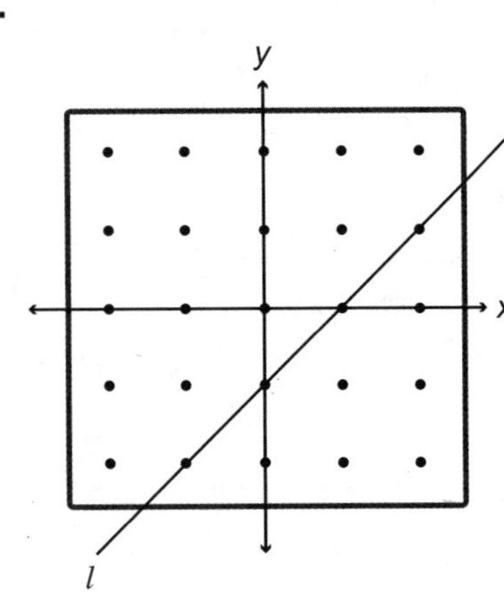

2.

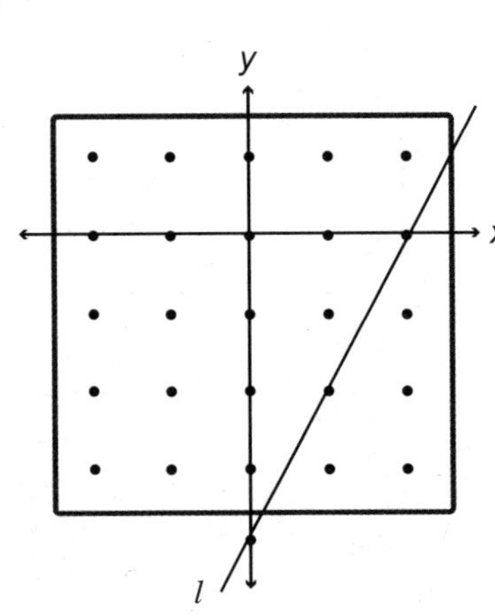

3.

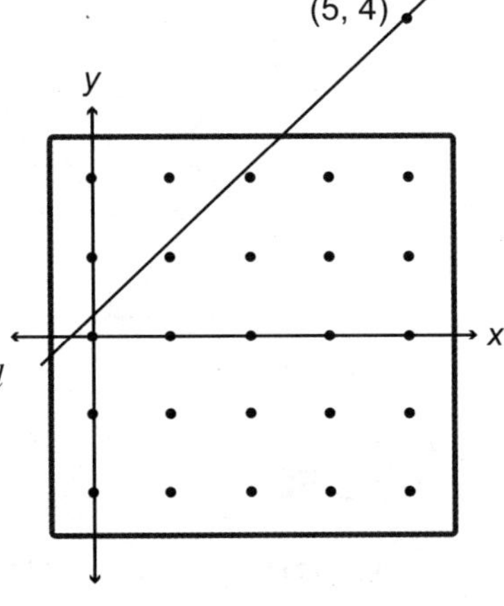

Page 62:

1. $m = \frac{3}{2}$; $3x - 2y = 0$, or $3x = 2y$

2. $m = 1$; $x - y = 1$, or $y = x - 1$

3. $m = \frac{1}{2}$; $x - 2y = {}^-2$, or $2y = x + 2$

4. $m = 1$; $y = x$, or $x - y = 0$

5. $m = {}^-1$; $y = {}^-x$, or $x + y = 0$

Page 65:

1. 60 degrees
2. 120 degrees
3. 90 degrees
4. 30 degrees
5. The measure of the central angle equals the measure of the intercepted arc.

Page 66:

1. 60 degrees **2.** 30 degrees **3.** 45 degrees **4.** 75 degrees

5. The measure of the inscribed angle equals $\frac{1}{2}$ the measure of the central angle. The measure of the central angle equals the measure of the intercepted arc.

Page 67:

1–5. 180 degrees

Page 68:

1. 120 degrees **2.** 120 degrees **3.** 60 degrees **4.** 60 degrees

5. 150 degrees **6.** 60 degrees

Page 69:

1. a. 30 degrees b. 90 degrees c. 60 degrees

2. a. 75 degrees b. 45 degrees c. 60 degrees

3. a. 30 degrees b. 45 degrees c. 90 degrees d. 60 degrees

4. a. 30 degrees b. 75 degrees c. 45 degrees d. 150 degrees

Page 70:

1. Isosceles, right

2. Scalene, right

3. Equilateral, acute

4. Scalene, obtuse

5. Isosceles, right

6. Scalene, acute

Page 71:

1. a. $\frac{1}{2}$; b. 60 degrees; c. 60 degrees

2. Minor arc *AQ*

3. 30 degrees

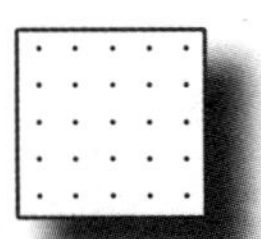

Answers (cont.)

Page 72:

1. True	**2.** True	**3.** False	**4.** True	**5.** True
6. False	**7.** False	**8.** False	**9.** False	**10.** False